Patchwork and Quilting
Book Number 2
Twenty projects by Kaffe Fassett
Liza Prior Lucy • Susan Powell • Karen Stone
Kim Hargreaves • Pauline Smith

A WESTMINSTER PRODUCTION

First Published in Great Britain in 2000 by
Rowan Yarns
Green Lane Mill
Holmfirth
West Yorkshire
England
HD7 1RW

Copyright Rowan Yarns 2000

Published in the U. S. A. by
Westminster Fibers Inc.
5 Northern Boulevard,
Amherst,
New Hampshire 03031
U. S. A.

Editor and text: Jane Bolsover
Art Director: Kim Hargreaves
Patchwork Designs: Kaffe Fassett, Liza Prior Lucy, Pauline Smith,
Kim Hargreaves, Susan Powell and Karen Stone
Quilters: Judy Irish and Bobbi Penniman
Photographer: Joey Toller
Design layout: Les Dunford
Techniques illustrations: Jane Bolsover
Patchwork instruction diagrams: Siriol Clarry
Sub Editor: Natalie Minnis

American Congress Library
Westminster Fibers
Patchwork and Quilting
IBSN 0-9672985-1-2

Colour reproduction by Chroma Graphics (Overseas) Pte. Ltd
Printed and bound in Singapore by KHL Printing Co. Pte. Ltd.

CONTENTS

INTRODUCTION

Welcome to Patchwork and Quilting book number two. Having just completed work on this publication, it is amazing how much we've evolved from our first book.

Firstly, it's very exciting that a number of other designers have joined Kaffe Fassett - Liza Prior Lucy, Pauline Smith, Kim Hargreaves, Karen Stone and Susan Powell - so there is a lot more variety on offer.

Susan Powell and Karen Stone are well established quiltmakers in the USA, and have inspired many people, including Liza Prior Lucy, to get more deeply involved in the craft of quiltmaking. With their extraordinary talent for appliquéd quilts, they've brought a new dimension to our book. Kim Hargreaves comes to us from the Rowan design team. Well known for her young contemporary sweater designs, Kim has translated her impeccable style beautifully into three new patchwork and quilting projects. Collectively the designers bring you an extended range of 22 projects - some simple, some challenging, but lots and lots of fun!

Just as exciting as new designers is the greatly increased size of the Kaffe Fassett Glorious Patchwork fabric range. There are some wonderful new prints, checks and stripes, but most importantly a range of plain shot cottons, in 28 delicious shades to add to existing ranges.

The story behind Kaffe's Patchwork fabric range is an interesting one. Each year he gives some time to assist artisans around the world, and the stripes, checks and plains in this range are all individually woven on simple hand looms, through the Fair Trading Trusts in India. Being hand-woven, this means that no two fabrics are identical, and the small imperfections that occur in the process all add to the inherent beauty of these cloths. This makes for some very exciting design possibilities, whether you're following our suggested colour recipes, or working out your own.

Finally, the book itself has been improved. The patchwork assembly instructions are now in full colour, making them clearer and easier to follow. You'll also find a swatch book section, so if you're confused by a fabric code, you can look it up at a glance.

We all hope that the creations within these pages give you the inspiration to take needle to hand and make something exciting.

Jane Bolsover

Jane Bolsover, Editor

Sunburst by Karen Stone
The instructions are not included for 'Sunburst', which is a
Foundation Piecing project. It comes as a single package containing
instructions and all of the foundation papers necessary to complete
the project. See page 30 for more information.

*This page Hush &
Ambrosia cushions
by Kim Hargreaves,
opposite Pale
Over Under Quilt
by Kaffe Fassett*

6

*This page
Lavender Cushion
by Kim Hargreaves
opposite Small
Diagonal Tablecloth
by Liza Prior Lucy*

9

This page Echo
Quilt and Hush
Cushion, opposite
Ambrosia cushion all
by Kim Hargreaves

10

Square Diamond Quilt by Pauline Smith

13

*This page
Psychedelic Flowers
by Karen Stone,
opposite Swatches
by Kaffe Fassett*

*This page Red Columns
Quilt, opposite African
Stripe Cushion both
by Kaffe Fassett*

This page African Stripe Baby Quilt, opposite Baby Pyramids Quilt both by Kaffe Fassett

This page Tote Bag
by Liza Prior Lucy,
opposite Boston
Common Tablecloth
by Kaffe Fassett

20

This page Square Diamond, Swatches & Amish Star Quilts, opposite Amish Star by Liza Prior Lucy

23

Dark Over Under Quilt by Kaffe Fassett

*Tiles Duvet Cover,
Pillow & Cushion all
by Pauline Smith*

*This page
assorted cushions,
opposite Grey
Columns Quilt
by Kaffe Fassett*

28

English Country Garden quilt by Susan Powell

English Country Garden quilt by Susan Powell and Sunburst by Karen Stone, see photograph on page 5, come as separate projects available from your local stockist.

English Country Garden quilt is sold as a BLOCK OF THE MONTH. There are twelve packages, sold separately, for each of the twelve months of the year. Every month you will be able to buy a package containing the pattern and instruction for that month. The first nine packages are the FLORAL BLOCKS, the tenth contains all the interesting details which fill the spaces between the Diamonds and the eleventh and twelfth are the BORDER packages.

Your local stockist of Kaffe Fassett fabrics will have all the packs and fabrics necessary for you to create a quilt as stunning as those of Karen Stone and Susan Powell.

Patchwork and Quilting Assembly Instructions

EXPERIENCE RATINGS

Pauline Smith

Square Diamond Quilt	★
Tiles Duvet Cover	★★
Tiles Pillowcase	★
Tiles Cushion	★

Kaffe Fassett

Swatches Quilt	★
Dark Over Under Quilt	★★★
Pale Over Under Quilt	★★★
Boston Common Tablecloth	★
African Stripe Baby Quilt	★
African Stripe Cushion	★
Red Columns Quilt	★★★
Grey Columns Quilt	★★★
Baby Pyramids Quilt	★★★

Liza Prior Lucy

Small Diagonal Tablecloth	★★
Tote Bag	★★
Amish Star Quilt	★★

Kim Hargreaves

Ambrosia Cushion	★
Hush and Lavender Cushions	★
Echo Quilt	★★

Karen Stone

Psychedelic Flowers	
Wall Hanging	★★★

KEY

★ Easy, straightforward, suitable for a beginner.

★★ Suitable for the average patchworker and quilter.

★★★ For the more experienced patchworker and quilter.

ABBREVIATIONS
The Kaffe Fassett Fabric collection

The Kaffe Fassett fabrics are available at Rowan stockists in Europe and the Far East. In USA, Canada and Australia they are available through Westminster stockists and better fabric stores.

Stripes

NS	Narrow stripe
PS	Pachrangi stripe
ES	Exotic stripe
AS	Alternate stripe
BS	Broad stripe
OS	Ombre stripe
BWS	Blue and white stripe

Checks

NC	Narrow check
BC	Broad check
EC	Exotic check

Prints

GP 01	Roman Glass
GP 02	Damask
GP 03	Gazania
GP 04	Beads
GP 06	Pebble Beach
GP 07	Artichokes
GP 08	Forget Me Not Rose
GP 09	Chard
GP 11	Flower Lattice
PR	Pressed Roses

Print colour numbers

L	Leafy
J	Jewel
S	Stones
C	Circus
P	Pastel
R	Red
BW	Blue and White
PK	Pink
G	Gold

Shot Cottons

SC 01	Ginger
SC 02	Cassis
SC 03	Prune
SC 04	Slate
SC 05	Opal
SC 06	Thunder
SC 07	Persimmon
SC 08	Raspberry
SC 09	Pomegranate
SC 10	Bittersweet
SC 11	Tangerine
SC 12	Chartreuse
SC 13	Navy
SC 14	Lavender
SC 15	Denim Blue
SC 16	Mustard
SC 17	Sage
SC 18	Tobacco
SC 19	Lichen
SC 20	Smoky
SC 21	Pine
SC 22	Pewter
SC 23	Stone Grey
SC 24	Ecru
SC 25	Charcoal
SC 26	Duck Egg
SC 27	Grass
SC 28	Blush

Fat Quarter

FQ	a 22½in x 20in (57cm x 50cm) piece of fabric sold as a Fat quarter

Square Diamond Quilt

PAULINE SMITH

When arranging the blocks in this quilt, it is more interesting if you place the striped square directions randomly, creating an effect rather as if they're floating. This project can easily be scaled up or down to fit a larger or smaller bed, by simply adding or subtracting blocks. Make up the central panel first and then measure for the border sizes.

SIZE OF QUILT
The finished quilt will measure approximately 78in x 88in (198cm x 224cm).

MATERIALS
Patchwork fabrics
BC 02: ⅔yd (60cm) or 3FQ
ES 23: ¼yd (23cm) or 1FQ
EC 03: ½yd (45cm) or 1FQ
NS 08: see backing fabric
NC 05: ⅔yd (60cm) or 2 FQ
SC 15: 1yd (90cm) or 4FQ

SC 18: 1yd (90cm) or 3FQ
SC 19: see outer border fabric
SC 20: see binding fabric
Inner border:
NS 08: see backing fabric
Outer border:
SC 19: 2yds (1.8m) or 8FQ
Backing fabric:
NS 08: 6⅔yd (6.1m)
Binding fabric:
SC 20: 2yds (1.8m) or 8FQ
Batting:
84in x 96in (214cm x 244cm)

Quilting thread:
Toning coloured embroidery, or fine crotchet cotton.

PATCH SHAPES
The quilt centre is made from blocks of one square (template A) and 4 triangles (template B). See page 77 for templates.

Templates

A   B

CUTTING OUT
Centre blocks group A:
Template A: Cut 4in- (10cm-) wide strips across width of fabric. Each strip will give you 11 patches per 45in- (114cm-) wide fabric, or 5 per FQ (see page 69). Cut 52 in BC 02.
Template B: Cut 3⅜in- (8.5cm-) wide strips across width of fabric. Each strip will give you 26 patches per 45cm- (114cm-) wide fabric, or 12 per FQ. Cut 208 in SC 15.
Centre blocks group B:
Template A: Cut 21 in ES 23.
Template B: Cut 84 in SC 20.
Centre blocks group C:
Template A: Cut 28 in NC 05.
Template B: Cut 112 in SC 19.
Centre blocks group D:
Template A: Cut 24 in EC 03.
Template B: Cut 96 in SC 18.
Centre blocks group E:
Template A: Cut 25 in NS 08.
Template B: Cut 100 in SC 20.
Centre blocks group F:
Template A: Cut 24 in NS 08.
Template B: Cut 96 in SC 19.
Centre blocks group G:
Template A: Cut 21 in NC 05.
Template B: Cut 84 in SC 18.
Inner borders:
Cut 3 end strips and 4 side strips, 3in- (7.5cm-) wide x width of fabric, in NS 08.
Outer borders:
Cut 4 end strips and four side strips, 4½in- (11.5cm-) wide x width of fabric in SC 19.
Straight grain binding:
Cut 9½yds x 4½in- (8.7m x 11.5cm-) wide in SC 20.

Quilt assembly

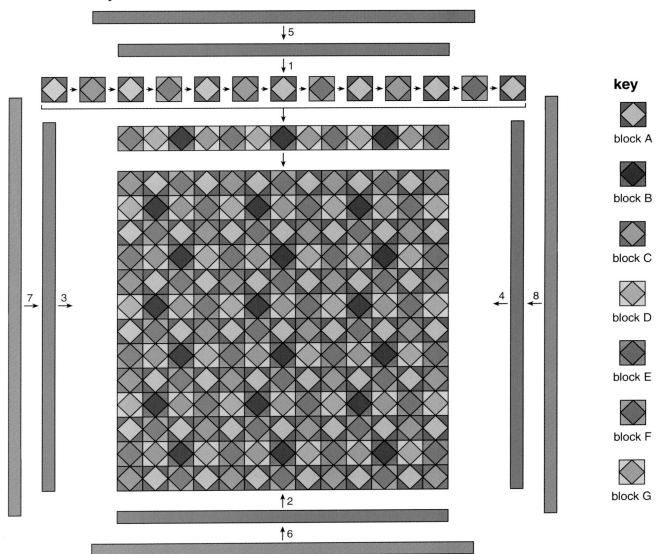

key

block A

block B

block C

block D

block E

block F

block G

Backing:
Cut 2 pieces 45in x 84in (114cm x 213cm), and 3 pieces 28½in x 5½in (72cm x 14cm) in NS 08.

MAKING THE BLOCKS
Using a ¼in (6mm) seam allowance make up 52- A blocks, 21- B blocks, 28- C blocks, 24- D blocks, 25- E blocks, 24- F blocks and 21- G blocks, following the block assembly diagram.

Block assembly

ASSEMBLING THE BLOCKS
Arrange the 195 blocks into 15 rows of 13 blocks following the quilt assembly diagram. Using a ¼in (6mm) seam allowance, join the blocks together into rows, then join the rows together to form the quilt top.

MAKING THE BORDERS
Join the inner border end strips to form 2 strips 65½in (166cm) long and the inner border side strips to form 2 strips 80½in (204.5cm) long. Attach the 2 end borders to the edges of the quilt and then the side borders. Repeat the same order with the outer borders, forming 2 end strips 70½in (179cm) long and 2 side strips 88½in (225cm) long.

FINISHING THE QUILT
Press the assembled quilt top. Seam the 5 backing pieces together with a ⅜in (1cm) seam allowance to form 1 piece measuring approximately 84in x 96in (214cm x 244cm). Layer the quilt top, batting and backing, and baste together (see page 71). Hand quilt a row of stitching, ¾in (2cm) in from the seam line, around each plain fabric diamond, formed at the joining of 4 plain triangles (see diagram below).
Trim the quilt edges and attach the binding (see page 72).

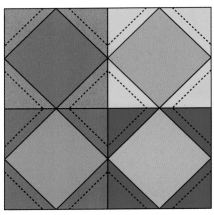

Quilting

33

Tiles Duvet Cover

PAULINE SMITH

B lue and white floor tiles were the spark of inspiration behind the design of this duvet cover. Pauline has given this project a 2 star rating, not because the patchwork is difficult to make, but because careful handling is required so as not to stretch the bias edges and distort the square blocks out of shape.

SIZE OF DUVET COVER

The finished single duvet cover will measure approximately 54in x 74in (138cm x 188cm); the double 84in x 74in (214cm x 188cm).

MATERIALS

Patchwork fabrics:
NC 02: Single: ⅛yd (15cm) or 1FQ
        Double: ½yd (45cm) or 2FQ
SC 05: Single: 1yd (90cm) or 4FQ
        Double: 1⅔yds (1.5m) or 7FQ
SC 06: Single: ⅓yd (30cm) or 1FQ
        Double: ½yd (45cm) or 2FQ

SC 08: Single: ⅛yd (15cm) or 1FQ
        Double: ⅛yd (15cm) or 1FQ
SC 15: Single: ⅛yd (15cm) or 1FQ
        Double: ¼yd (23cm) or 1FQ
SC 20: Single: ⅔yd (60cm) or 2FQ
        Double: ¾yd (70cm) or 3FQ
BWS 02: see backing fabric

Borders and facings:
BWS 02: see backing fabric

Backing:
BWS 02: Single: 5½yds (5m)
         Double: 7¾yds (7.1m)

Buttons:
Single bed: 4 x 22mm
Double bed: 6 x 22mm

PATCH SHAPES

The Duvet top is made from 2 different blocks. Block 1 is formed by 1square (template A), 4 small triangles (template C), 4 medium triangles (template E) and 4 large triangles (template D).

Block 2 is formed by 1 small square (template F), 4 tiny triangles (template J), 4 rectangles (template G), 4 medium triangles (template I), and 4 small triangles (template H). See pages 76 & 77 for the templates.

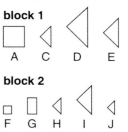

Templates

block 1

A   C   D   E

block 2

F   G   H   I   J

CUTTING OUT

Block 1

Template A: Cut 4in- (10cm-) wide strips across width of fabric. Each strip will give you 11 patches per 45in- (114cm-) wide fabric, or 5 per FQ (see page 69). Cut 18 for a single bed, 28 for a double in NC 02.

Template C: Cut 3⅜in- (8.5cm-) wide strips across width of fabric. Each strip will give you 26 patches per 45in- (114cm-) wide fabric, or 12 per FQ (see page 69). Cut 72 for a single bed, 112 for a double in SC 06.

Template D: Cut 72 for a single bed, 112 for a double in BWS 02, making sure stripes are running the correct way.

Template E: Cut 4⅜in- (11.25cm-) wide strips across width of fabric. Each strip will give you 20 patches per 45in- (114cm-) wide fabric, or 10 per FQ. Cut 72 for a single bed, 112 for a double in SC 20.

Block 2

Template F: Cut 2⅝in- (6.5cm-) wide strips across width of fabric. Each strip will give you 17 patches per 45in- (114cm-) wide fabric, or 8 per FQ.

Duvet top assembly

key

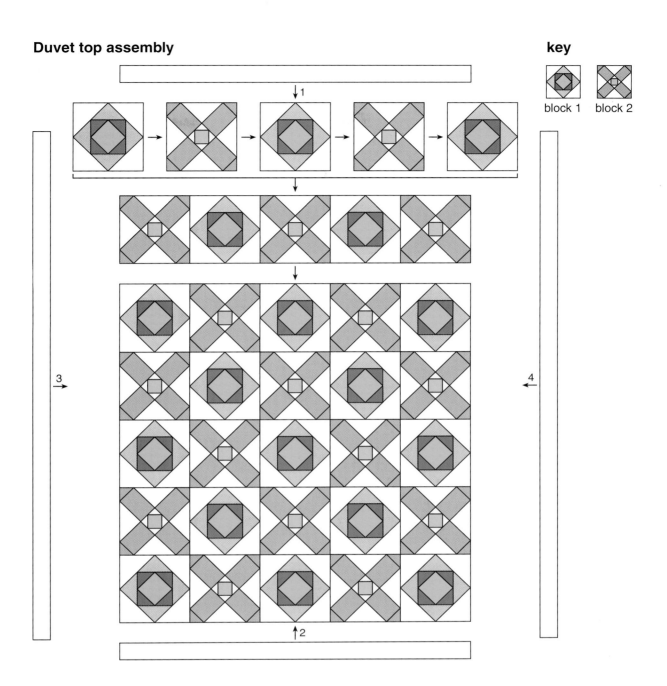

block 1   block 2

Cut 17 for a single bed, 28 for a double in SC 08.

Template G: Cut 4⅝in- (11.5cm-) wide strips across width of fabric. Each strip will give you 12 patches per 45in- (114cm-) wide fabric, or 6 per FQ. Cut 68 for a single bed, 112 for a double in SC 05.

Template H: Cut 3in- (7.5cm-) wide strips across width of fabric. Each strip will give you 30 patches per 45in- (114cm-) wide fabric, or 14 per FQ. Cut 68 for a single bed, 112 for a double in SC 05.

Template I: Cut 68 for a single bed, 112 for a double in BWS 02, making sure stripes are running the correct way.

Template J: Cut 2⅜in- (6cm-) wide strips across width of fabric. Each strip

will give you 38 patches per 45in- (114cm-) wide fabric, or 18 per FQ. Cut 68 for a single bed, 112 for a double bed in SC 15.

Borders:
For a single bed cut 2 end strips 50½in x 2½in (128cm x 6.5cm), and 2 side strips 74½in x 2½in (189cm x 6.5cm) in BWS 02, with stripes down length. For a double bed cut 2 end strips 80½in x 2½in (204cm x 6.5cm), and 2 side strips 74½in x 2½in (189cm x 6.5cm) in BWS 02, with stripes down length.

Backing:
For a single bed, cut 2 pieces in BWS 02, 37½in x 54½in (95cm x 138cm). For a double bed, cut 2 pieces in BWS 02, 37½in x 84½in (95cm x 215cm). Note: the stripes will run across the width of

the duvet cover when completed.
Facings:
For a single bed, cut 2 strips across the width of the fabric 27½in x 2½in (70cm x 6.5cm), and 2 strips 27½in x 5in (70cm x 12.5cm) in BWS 02. For a double bed, cut 2 strips 42½in x 2½in (108cm x 6.5cm), and 2 strips 42½in x 5in (108cm x 12.5cm) in BWS 02.

MAKING THE BLOCKS
Single bed: Using a ¼in (6mm) seam allowance make up 18 of block 1 and 17 of block 2, following the block assembly diagrams (see page 36).

Double bed: Using a ¼in (6mm) seam allowance make up 28 of block 1 and 28 of block 2, following the block assembly diagrams (see page 36).

Block 1 assembly

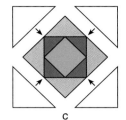

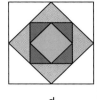

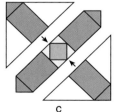

Block 2 assembly

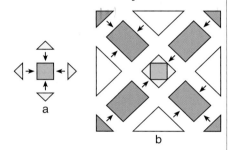

ASSEMBLING THE BLOCKS

Single bed: Arrange 35 blocks alternately into 7 rows of 5 blocks, following the assembly diagram, see previous page.
Double bed: Arrange the 56 blocks alternately into 7 rows of 8 blocks, using the assembly diagram as a guide. Using a ¼in (6mm) seam allowance, join the blocks together into rows, then join the rows together to form the duvet top.

MAKING THE BORDERS AND FACINGS

Attach the two end borders to the edges of the patchwork top, and then the side borders. Join the two narrower facing pieces together to form a strip 54½in (138cm) long for a single bed, and 84½in (215cm) for a double. Repeat with the wider facing strips.

COMPLETING THE DUVET

For full instructions on how to complete the duvet cover, turn to page 73 in the Patchwork Know-how section.

Boston Common Tablecloth ★

KAFFE FASSETT

Kaffe designed this project whilst working in Stratford-Upon-Avon, on the costumes and sets for Shakespeare's play 'As You Like It'. He saw a photograph of a traditional 'one patch' American quilt from the 1930s. Inspired by this, he scaled down the idea to produce this brightly coloured tablecloth, which would make a great accompaniment to any table.

SIZE OF TABLECLOTH

The finished tablecloth will measure approx. 38½in x 38½in (98cm x 98cm).

MATERIALS
Patchwork fabrics:
OS 01: ⅛yd (15cm) or 1FQ
OS 05: see backing fabric
PR 01: ⅓yd (30cm) or 2FQ
PR 02: ⅛yd (15cm) or 1FQ
PR 03: ⅛yd (15cm) or 1FQ
PR 04: ⅛yd (15cm) or 1FQ
PR 05: ⅛yd (15cm) or 1FQ
PR 06: ⅛yd (15cm) or 1FQ
PR 07: see binding fabric
GP 01-G: ⅛yd (15cm) or 1FQ
GP 01-BW: ¼yd (23cm) or 1FQ
GP 01-PK: ⅛yd (15cm) or 1FQ
GP 01-S: ¼yd (23cm) or 1FQ
GP 06-J: ⅛yd (15cm) or 1FQ
NC 01: ⅛yd (15cm) or 1FQ
PS 04: ⅛yd (15cm) or 1FQ

Tablecloth assembly

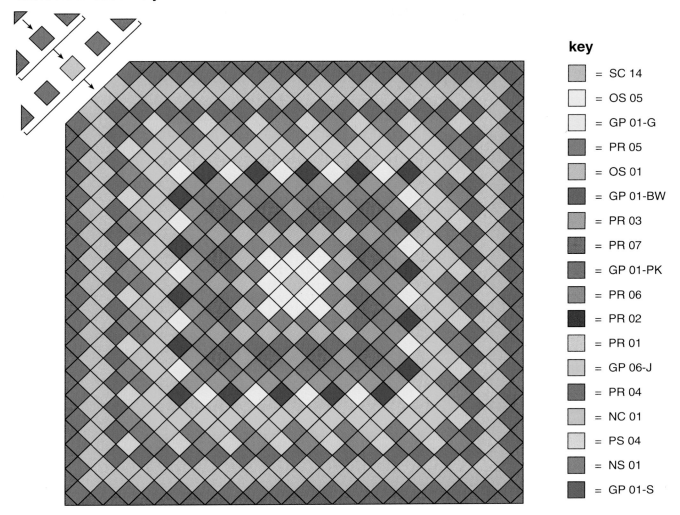

key

=	SC 14
=	OS 05
=	GP 01-G
=	PR 05
=	OS 01
=	GP 01-BW
=	PR 03
=	PR 07
=	GP 01-PK
=	PR 06
=	PR 02
=	PR 01
=	GP 06-J
=	PR 04
=	NC 01
=	PS 04
=	NS 01
=	GP 01-S

NS 01: $\frac{1}{8}$yd (15cm) or 1FQ
SC 14: $\frac{1}{4}$yd (23cm) or 1FQ
Backing fabric:
OS 05: 1$\frac{1}{4}$yds (1.2m)
Binding fabric:
PR 07: $\frac{2}{3}$yd (60cm) or 3FQ

PATCH SHAPES

The tablecloth top is made from 1 main patch shape: a small square (template CC), and the border is made from 2 patch shapes: a small triangle (template DD) and a tiny triangle (template EE). See page 78 for templates.

Templates

CC   DD   EE

CUTTING OUT

Template CC: Cut 2in- (5cm-) wide strips across width of fabric. Each strip will give you 22 patches per 45in- (114cm-) wide fabric, or 11 per FQ (see page 69). Cut 4 in OS 05. Cut 12 in PR 03, PR 05 and PR 07. Cut 16 in OS 01 and 18 in PR 02. Cut 24 in PR 04 and NC 01. Cut 26 in PS 04, NS 01and GP 01-G. Cut 28 in GP 01-PK and 32 in PR 06. Cut 44 in GP 06-J and 56 in GP 01-S. Cut 65 in SC 14 and 88 in GP 01-BW. Cut 100 in PR 01.
Template DD: Cut 2$\frac{3}{8}$in- (6cm-) wide strips across width of fabric. Each strip will give you 38 patches per 45in- (114cm-) wide fabric, or 18 per FQ. Cut 68 in PR 07.
Template EE: Cut 4 in PR 07.
Binding:
Cut 4 strips 2$\frac{1}{2}$in- (6cm-) wide x width of fabric in PR 07, to form 4$\frac{1}{2}$yds (4.1m) of binding.

Backing:
Cut 1 piece 38$\frac{1}{2}$in x 38$\frac{1}{2}$in (98cm x 98cm) in OS 05.

ASSEMBLING THE PATCHWORK TOP

Arrange the square patches into 35 diagonal rows, following the quilt assembly diagram. Place a small triangle at each end of each row, making sure it is facing the correct direction. Using a $\frac{1}{4}$in (6mm) seam allowance, join the patches into rows, and then the rows together to form the tablecloth top. Stitch a tiny triangle to each corner of the tablecloth to complete the top.

FINISHING THE TABLECLOTH

Press the assembled tablecloth top. Layer the cloth top and backing, and baste together (see page 71). Attach binding to edges (see page 72).

Tiles Pillowcase

PAULINE SMITH

Templates

☐ ◸
F   J

CUTTING OUT

Corner blocks
Template F: cut 4 in SC 08.
Template J: cut 16 in SC 15.
Borders:
Cut 2 strips 14½in x 3½in (37cm x 9cm) in SC 05.
Front:
Cut 1 piece with the stripes running along the long edges, 23½in x 20½in (60cm x 52cm) in BWS 02.
Back:
Cut 1 piece with the stripes running along the long edges, 36in x 20½in (90cm x 52cm) in BWS 02.
Facing:
Cut 1 strip with the stripes running along the long edges, 20½in x 3½in (52cm x 9cm).

Block assembly

This charming pillowcase has been designed to go with the Tiles duvet cover. The borders are made from a straight strip, combined with corner blocks taken from the centre of the duvet cover block 2. Please note, the fabric quantities given here are for making one pillowcase only.

MAKING THE BORDERS

Using a ¼in (6mm) seam allowance, make up 4 blocks, following the assembly diagram. Then attach 1 block to each end of the border strips, using a ¼in (6mm) seam allowance.

SIZE OF PILLOWCASE

The finished pillowcase will measure approximately. 29in x 20in (74cm x 51cm).

MATERIALS

Patchwork fabrics:
SC 08: ⅛yd (15cm) or 1FQ, or use remainder from duvet cover
SC 15: ⅛yd (15cm) or 1FQ

Border fabric:
SC 05: ⅛yd (15cm) or 1FQ
Back, front and facing:
BWS 02: 1⅛yd (1.1m)

PATCH SHAPES

The border corners are made from block formed by a small square (template F) and 4 tiny triangles (template J). See page 76 for the templates.

Border assembly

MAKING THE PILLOWCASE

Stitch a border strip to each short side edge of the front pillowcase. For full instructions on how to complete the pillowcase, turn to page 73 in the Patchwork Know-how section.

Tiles Cushion

PAULINE SMITH

★

Batting:
20in x20in (51cm x 51cm).
Cushion pad:
17½in x 17½in (45cm x 45cm)
Quilting threads:
Raspberry and slate coloured machine quilting thread

PATCH SHAPES

The cushion top is made by using block 1 from the Tiles duvet cover. Block 1 is formed by 1 square (template A), 4 small triangles (template C), 4 medium triangles (template E), and 4 larger triangles (template D). See page 77 for templates. The outer corners of the cushion top are bordered by 4 large triangles (template K). You'll find half of this template on page 77. Place fold edge of template to fold of paper. Trace around shape and cut out double thickness. Open out to complete template.

Templates

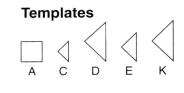

A   C   D   E   K

Continuing the floor tiles theme, Pauline has designed a cushion, using 1 block from the duvet, edged with a simple border and large triangles, which twist the block around into a diamond. This project is a good way to use up scraps left over from the bed linen, and of course it looks great when placed on the bed for decoration.

SIZE OF CUSHION COVER
The finished cushion cover will measure approximately 17in x 17in (44cm x 44cm).

MATERIALS
Patchwork fabrics:
NC 02: see backing fabrics
SC 06: see backing fabrics

SC 20: ⅛yd (15cm) or 1FQ
BWS 02: ¼yd (23cm) or 1FQ
Inner border and binding:
SC 08: ⅛yd (15cm) or 1FQ
Cushion backs:
SC 06: ⅓yd (30cm) or 1FQ
NC 02: ⅓yd (30cm) or 1FQ
Lining:
⅔yd (60cm) x 45in- (114cm-) wide lining

CUTTING OUT
Block 1
Template A: cut 1 in NC 02.
Template C: cut 4 in SC 06.
Template D: cut 4 in BWS 02, making sure stripes are running the correct way.
Template E: cut 4 in SC 20.
Inner borders:
Cut 2 end strips 10½in x 1½in (27cm x 4cm), and 2 side strips 12½in x 1½in (32cm x 4cm) in SC 08.
Corners:
Template K: cut 4 in SC 06.
Cushion backs:
Cut 1 piece 17½in x 10in (44.5cm x 25.5cm) in SC 06, and 1 piece in NC 02.
Binding:
Cut 2 strips 17½in x 2½in (44.5cm x 6.5cm) in SC 08.
Lining:
Cut 1 piece 20in x 20in (51cm x 51cm).

MAKING THE CUSHION TOP

Using a ¼in (6mm) seam allowance, make up the block 1, following the assembly diagram for the Tiles duvet cover. Then, attach the borders and large triangular corners following the Cushion top assembly diagram.

Cushion top assembly

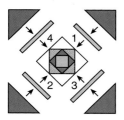

QUILTING THE TOP

Press assembled cushion top. Layer top, batting and lining, and baste together (see page 71). Stitch-in-the-ditch around each patch, then free-motion quilt the blue and white striped sections with a slate coloured thread, and the large corner triangles with a raspberry coloured thread, using the quilting diagrams as a guide. Trim the batting and lining edges level with cushion top.

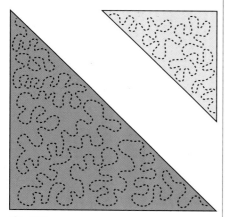

Quilting

FINISHING OFF THE COVER

For full instructions on how to complete the cushion cover, turn to page 73 in the Patchwork Know-how section.

African Stripe Cushion

★

KAFFE FASSETT

This project is a much more colourful version of the African Ashanti weaving (see African Stripe Baby Quilt, page 52). Kaffe has used a large variety of fabrics to produce this design, but you could always substitute some of the horizontal stripes with remnants from other projects. Always keep the stripes running the correct way, in order to retain the woven effect.

SIZE OF CUSHION

The finished cushion will measure approximately 28½in x 28½in (73cm x 73cm).

MATERIALS

Patchwork fabrics:
BC 01: ⅛yd (15cm) or 1FQ
BC 04: see backing fabrics
AS 10: ⅛yd (15cm) or 1FQ
AS 21: ¼yd (23cm) or 1FQ
BS 01: see backing fabrics
BS 11: see backing fabrics
PS 04: ⅛yd (15cm) or 1FQ
PS 13: ¼yd (23cm) or 1FQ
PS 14: ¼yd (23cm) or 1FQ
PS 22: see backing fabrics
Border and binding fabrics:
SC 02: ¼yd (23cm) or 1FQ
SC 18: ¼yd (23cm) or 1FQ

40

Cushion assembly

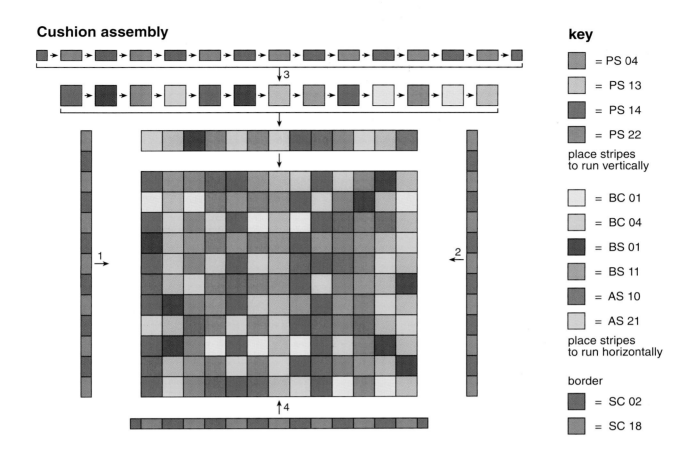

key

- ☐ = PS 04
- ☐ = PS 13
- ☐ = PS 14
- ☐ = PS 22

place stripes
to run vertically

- ☐ = BC 01
- ☐ = BC 04
- ☐ = BS 01
- ☐ = BS 11
- ☐ = AS 10
- ☐ = AS 21

place stripes
to run horizontally

border

- ☐ = SC 02
- ☐ = SC 18

Backing fabrics:
BC 04: ½yd (45cm) or 1FQ
BS 01: ½yd (45cm) or 1FQ
BS 11: ½yd (45cm) or 1FQ
PS 22: ½yd (45cm) or 1FQ
Cushion pad:
29½in x 29½in (75cm x 75cm)

PATCH SHAPES

This main cushion top is made from 1 small square (template BB), and the borders are made from a small rectangle (template FF) and a tiny square (template GG). See page 78 for templates.

Templates

BB   FF   GG

CUTTING OUT

Vertical stripes:
Template BB: Cut 2½in- (6.5cm-) wide strips across width of fabric. Each strip will give you 18 patches per 45in- (114cm-) wide fabric, or 9 per FQ (see page 69). Cut 13 in PS 04, 19 in PS 22,

26 in PS 13 and 27 in PS 14.
Horizontal stripes:
Template BB: Cut 8 in BC 04, 11 in BS 01, 12 in BC 01, 16 in AS 10, 17 in BS 11 and 20 in AS 21.
Borders:
Template FF: Cut 1¾in- (4.5cm-) wide strips across width of fabric. Each strip will give you 18 patches per 45in- (114cm-) wide fabric, or 9 per FQ. Cut 24 in SC 02 and 28 in SC 18.
Template GG: Cut 4 in SC 02.
Cushion backs:
Cut 1 piece 14¾in x 18½in (38cm x 47cm) in BS 01, BC 04, PS 22 and BS 11.
Binding squares:
Template BB: Cut 14 in SC 18 and 16 in SC 02.

ASSEMBLING THE CUSHION TOP

Arrange the 169 squares into 13 rows of 13 patches, following the cushion assembly diagram for both colour and stripes positioning. Using a ¼in (6mm) seam allowance, join the patches into rows, and then join the rows to form the cushion top.

ASSEMBLING THE BORDERS

Arrange 4 rows of 13 patches, using the assembly diagram as a guide. Join patches together into 4 separate rows. To form the end borders attach a tiny square to each end of 2 border rows. Attach the 2 side borders to the edges of the cushion top, and then the end borders.

ASSEMBLING THE BINDING

Arrange 2 rows of 13 patches arranging the colours alternately. Using a ¼in (6mm) seam allowance, join the patches into 2 separate rows.

FINISHING OFF THE COVER

Press the assembled cushion top and binding strips. Using a ⅜in (1cm) seam allowance, join 2 cushion backs to form 1 piece measuring approximately 18½in x 28½in (47cm x 72cm). Repeat with the remaining 2 backs. For full instructions on how to complete the cushion cover, turn to page 73 in the Patchwork Know-how section.

41

Swatches Quilt

KAFFE FASSETT

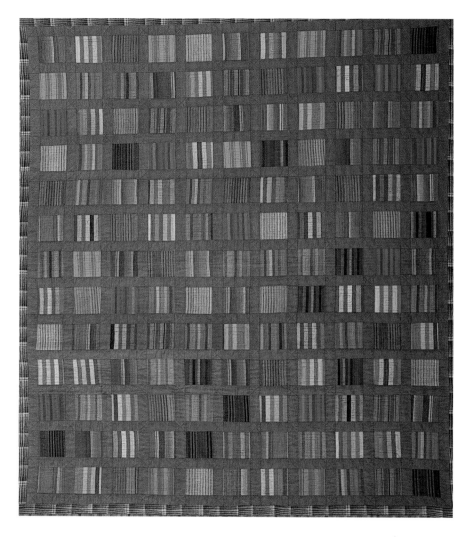

T he subtlety of colours in a swatch book gave the inspiration for this quilt. However, don't feel you have to buy all the fabrics suggested for this project - you could use fewer fabric choices, or more. It's an ideal way of using up your scraps.

SIZE OF QUILT
The finished quilt will measure approximately 75in x 64in (190cm x 163cm).

MATERIALS
Patchwork fabrics:
ES 10: ⅛yd (15cm) or 1FQ
ES 15: ⅓yd (30cm) or 1FQ
ES 21: ⅛yd (15cm) or 1FQ
AS 01: ⅛yd (15cm) or 1FQ
AS 10: ⅛yd (15cm) or 1FQ
NS 01: ⅛yd (15cm) or 1FQ

NS 08: ⅛yd (15cm) or 1FQ
NS 09: ⅛yd (15cm) or 1FQ
NS 13: see binding fabric
NS 17: ⅓yd (30cm) or 1FQ
PS 01: ⅛yd (15cm) or 1FQ
PS 04: ⅛yd (15cm) or 1FQ
PS 13: ⅛yd (15cm) or 1FQ
PS 15: ⅛yd (15cm) or 1FQ
PS 22: ⅛yd (15cm) or 1FQ
BS 01: ⅓yd (30cm) or 1FQ
BS 06: ⅓yd (30cm) or 1FQ
BS 23: ⅓yd (30cm) or 1FQ
SC 22: 2yds (1.8m) or 9FQ

Border fabric:
EC 01: ⅔yd (60cm)
Backing fabric:
BC 02: 4yds (3.7m)
Binding fabric:
NS 13: ¾yd (70cm)
Batting:
80in x 70in (200cm x 180cm)
Quilting thread:
Pewter coloured machine quilting thread

PATCH SHAPES
The quilt centre is made from one block, formed with large square (template X), a short rectangle (template Y), and a long rectangle (template Z). The lower edge of the centre is made from a small square (template AA) and the short rectangle (template Y). See pages 76 & 79 for templates.

Templates

X   Y   Z   AA

CUTTING OUT
Template X: Cut 4½in- (11.5cm-) wide strips across width of fabric. Each strip will give you 9 patches per 45in- (114cm-) wide fabric, or 4 per FQ (see page 69). Cut 5 in PS 13, 6 in PS 15, PS 22, NS 09, NS 13 and ES 21, 7 in PS 01, PS 04, AS 01, AS 10 and ES 10, 8 in NS 08, 9 in NS 01, 10 in BS 06 and NS 17, 11 in BS 23, 12 in ES 15 and 13 in BS 01.
Template Y: Cut 4½in- (11.5cm-) wide strips across width of fabric. Each strip will give you 22 patches per 45in- (114cm-) wide fabric, or 11 per FQ. Cut 154 in SC 22.
Template Z: Cut 6in- (15.25cm-) wide strips across width of fabric. Each strip will give you 22 patches per 45in- (114cm-) wide fabric, or 11 per FQ. Cut 156 in SC 22.
Template AA: Cut 12 in SC 22.
Borders: For the side borders, cut 4 strips 2¼in- (6cm-) wide x 35¾in (91cm) in EC 01. For the end borders, cut 4 strips 2¼in- (6cm-) wide x 32½in (82.5cm) in EC 01.
Straight cut binding:
Cut 7 strips 2½in- (6.5cm-) wide x width of fabric in NS 13, to form 8yds (7.3m) of binding.

Quilt assembly

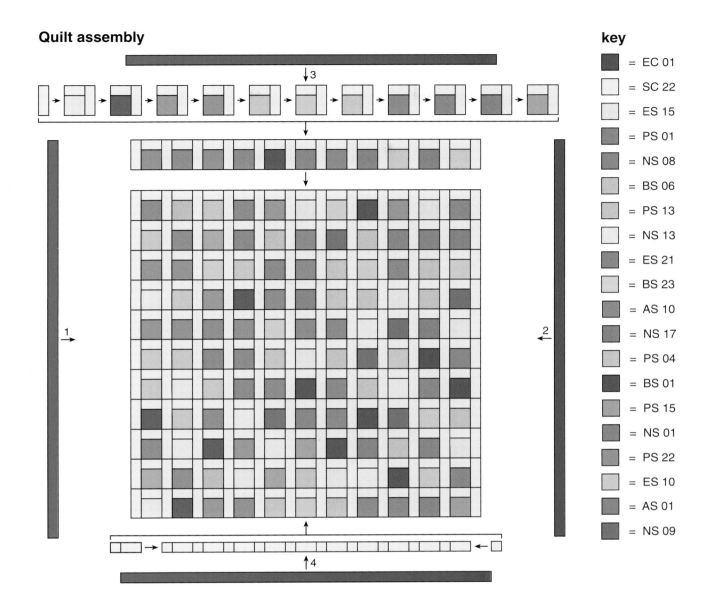

key

■	= EC 01
□	= SC 22
□	= ES 15
■	= PS 01
■	= NS 08
□	= BS 06
□	= PS 13
□	= NS 13
■	= ES 21
□	= BS 23
■	= AS 10
■	= NS 17
□	= PS 04
■	= BS 01
□	= PS 15
□	= NS 01
■	= PS 22
□	= ES 10
■	= AS 01
■	= NS 09

Backing:
Cut 2 pieces 41in x 70in (104cm x 178cm) in BC 02.

Block assembly

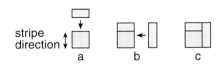

stripe direction

a   b   c

Lower inner border block

a   b

MAKING THE BLOCKS
Following the block assembly diagrams, make up 143 blocks, making sure that the square stripes (template X) run parallel to the long rectangles (template Z), and use a ¼in (6mm) seam allowance. Make up 11 lower inner border blocks, following the assembly diagrams.

ASSEMBLING THE BLOCKS
Arrange the 143 blocks into 13 rows of 11 blocks and arrange 1 row of lower inner border blocks following the quilt assembly diagram. Using a ¼in (6mm) seam allowance, join the blocks into rows and attach an extra long rectangle to the left hand end of each row, and an extra small square to the right hand end of the lower inner border, as shown. Join the rows together to form the quilt top.

MAKING THE BORDERS
Using a ¼in (6mm) seam allowance join the end border strips to form 2 strips 71in x 2¼in (180cm x 6cm), and the side border strips to form 2 strips 64½in x 2¼in (164cm x 6cm). Attach the 2 side borders to the edges of the quilt top and then the end borders.

FINISHING THE QUILT
Press the assembled quilt top. Seam the 2 backing pieces together with a ⅜in (1cm) seam allowance to form 1 piece measuring approximately 80in x 70in (200cm x 180cm). Layer the quilt top, batting, and backing, and baste together (see page 71).
Using a toning thread, stitch-in-the-ditch around every patch shape (see page 71). Then stitch a square and cross shape on the plain border strips at the corners of each large square, and work a square spiral shape on each large striped square patch shape.
Trim the quilt edges and attach the binding (see page 72).

43

Dark Over Under Quilt

KAFFE FASSETT

SC 12: ⅛yd (15cm) or 1FQ
SC 14: ⅛yd (15cm) or 1FQ
SC 16: ⅛yd (15cm) or 1FQ
SC 20: ¼yd (23cm) or 1FQ
SC 21: ½yd (45cm) or 2FQ
SC 26: ¼yd (23cm) or 1FQ
AS 01: 1yd (90cm) or 4FQ

Backing fabric:
NS 13: 8yd (7.3m)

Binding fabric:
PS 15: 1yd (90cm)

Batting:
98in x 108in (250cm x 275cm)

Quilting thread:
Various colours of machine quilting threads.

PATCH SHAPES

The quilt top is made from 3 different sized blocks and an inner border block. Block A is formed with 4 large rectangles cut 8½in x 12½in (21.5cm x 32cm) and 1 large square (template L). Block B is made from 4 medium rectangles (template M) and 1 medium square (template N). Block C is made from 4 small rectangles (template O) and 1 small square (template P). The inner border blocks are made from 2 trapezoids (template Q) and 2 triangles (template R). See pages 78 & 79 for templates.

Templates

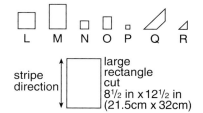

CUTTING OUT

Block A:
8½in x 12½in (21.5cm x 32cm) rectangles: Cut 4 in BS 01, BS 06 and BS 08.

Template L: Cut 1 in SC 07, SC 20 and SC 26.

Block B:
Template M: Cut 6½in- (16.5cm-) wide strips across width of fabric. Each strip will give you 9 patches per 45in- (114cm-) wide fabric, or 4 per FQ (see page 69). Cut 68 in NS 01, 32 in NS 08, 36 in NS 09, 44 in NS 13 and 28 in NS 17.

Template N: Cut 2 in SC 07 and SC 09, 3 in SC 01 and SC 20, 4 in

Kaffe loves playing with stripes and stripe directions to create wonderful kaleidoscopic effects. Here he's taken one simple block shape in 3 sizes, and has chosen the stripe widths to relate to the block sizes. The bright plain centres used for each block resemble little jewels – they really sparkle, rather like an Indian mirror embroidery.

SIZE OF QUILT

The finished quilt will measure approx. 90in x 100in (228cm x 254cm).

MATERIALS

Patchwork fabrics:
BS 01: ½yd (45cm) or 2FQ
BS 06: ½yd (45cm) or 2FQ
BS 08: ½yd (45cm) or 2FQ
NS 01: 1½yd (1.4m) or 6FQ
NS 08: ¾yd (70cm) or 3FQ
NS 09: ¾yd (70cm) or 3FQ

NS 13: see backing fabric
NS 17: ¾yd (70cm) or 3FQ
PS 01: ½yd (45cm) or 2FQ
PS 08: ¼yd (23cm) or 1FQ
PS 13: ⅓yd (30cm) or 2FQ
PS 15: see binding fabric
PS 22: 1⅓yds (1.2m) or 6FQ
SC 01: ⅛yd (15cm) or 1FQ
SC 07: ¼yd (23cm) or 1FQ
SC 08: ⅛yd (15cm) or 1FQ
SC 09: ⅛yd (15cm) or 1FQ
SC 11: ⅛yd (15cm) or 1FQ

44

Quilt assembly

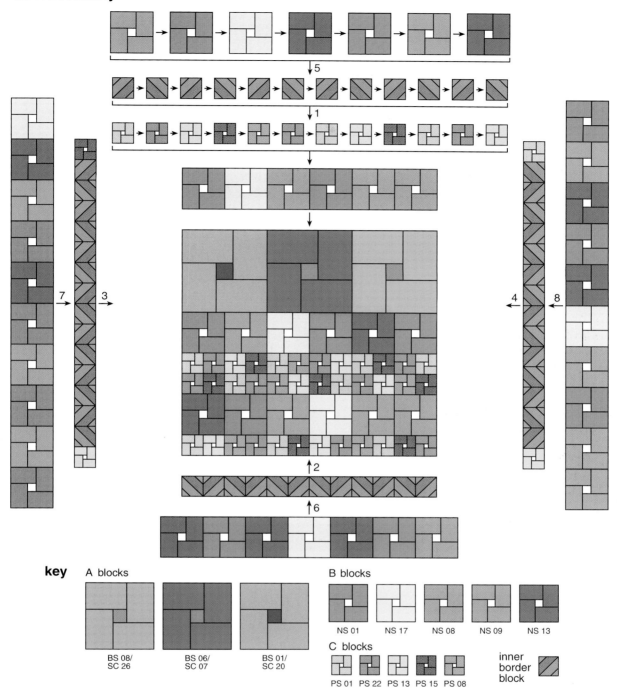

key

A blocks

BS 08/ SC 26

BS 06/ SC 07

BS 01/ SC 20

B blocks

NS 01   NS 17   NS 08   NS 09   NS 13

C blocks

PS 01   PS 22   PS 13   PS 15   PS 08

inner border block

SC 08, 5 in SC 11, SC 16 and SC 26, 7 in SC 14 and SC 21 and 9 in SC 12.

Block C:

Template O: Cut 3½in- (9cm-) wide strips across width of fabric. Each strip will give you 17 patches per 45in- (114cm-) wide fabric, or 8 per FQ. Cut 52 in PS 01, 24 in PS 08, 44 in PS 13, 40 in PS 15 and 48 in PS 22.

Template P: Cut 1 in SC 09, 2 in SC 07, 3 in SC 01 and SC 20, 4 in SC 11, 5 in SC 21 and SC 26, 6 in SC 08 and SC 12, 7 in SC 16 and 10 in SC 14.

Inner border blocks:

Template Q: Cut 8¼in- (21cm-) wide across width of fabric. Each strip will give you 16 patches per 45in- (114cm-) wide

fabric, or 8 per FQ. Cut 52 in AS 01 and PS 22.

Template R: Cut 104 in SC 21.

Straight grain binding:

Cut 9 strips 2½in- (6.5cm-) wide x width of fabric in PS 15, to form 10¾yd (9.7m) of binding.

Backing:

Cut 2 pieces 45in x 98in (114cm x 250cm), and 2 pieces 19in x 49½in (48cm x 126cm) in NS 13.

MAKING THE BLOCKS

Using a ¼in (6mm) seam allowance make up 3 A blocks, 52 B blocks and 52 C blocks following the block assembly diagrams and stitching between the dots

only, marked on the squares. Make up 52 inner border blocks following the assembly diagrams.

Border block assembly

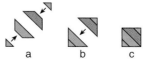

a   b   c

Block assembly

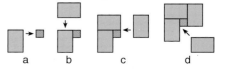

a   b   c   d

ASSEMBLING THE BLOCKS

Arrange the centre blocks into 8 rows of 12 C blocks, 6 B blocks, 3 A blocks, 6 B blocks, 12 C blocks, 12 C blocks, 6 B blocks and 12 C blocks following the quilt assembly diagram. Using a ¼in (6mm) seam allowance, join the blocks together into rows, then join the rows together to form the quilt centre.

For the end inner borders, arrange 2 rows of 12 inner border blocks following the quilt assembly diagram. For the side inner borders, arrange 2 rows of 14 inner border blocks, with 1 C block at each end. Join blocks together into the rows, then attach the end borders then the side borders. Following the quilt assembly diagram, arrange 2 rows of 7 B blocks to fit the ends of the quilt and 2 rows of 10 B blocks for the sides. Using a ¼in (6mm) seam allowance, join blocks together into rows, then attach them to the ends first, followed by the sides.

FINISHING THE QUILT

Press the assembled quilt top. Seam the backing pieces together with a ⅜in (1cm) seam allowance to form 1 piece 98in x 108in (249 x 275cm). Layer the quilt top, batting and backing, and baste together (see page 71).

Work a square row of machine quilting centrally around each B and C block, and 2 square rows spaced evenly apart, around each A block, using the quilting diagrams as a guide. Stitch-in-the-ditch diagonally across the centre of each inner border block, forming a zigzag line of quilting. Trim the quilt edges and attach the binding (see page 72).

block A

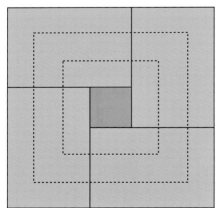

blocks B and C

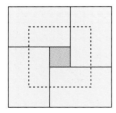

Quilting

Small Diagonal Tablecloth

LIZA PRIOR LUCY

★★

At first inspection this project looks like it's constructed in diagonal rows, but it's much simpler than that. The rows are made horizontally by inverting every other block.

SIZE OF TABLECLOTH

The finished tablecloth will measure approx. 40½in x 40½in (103cm x 103cm).

MATERIALS

Patchwork fabrics:
OS 01: see backing fabric
OS 02: ¼yd (23cm) or 2FQ
OS 04: ¼yd (23cm) or 2FQ
OS 05: ¼yd (23cm) or 2FQ
ES 20: ¼yd (23cm) or 1FQ
NS 01: ¼yd (23cm) or 1FQ
NS 13: ¼yd (23cm) or 1FQ
NS 16: see binding fabric
PS 04: ¼yd (23cm) or 1FQ
PS 22: ¼yd (23cm) or 1FQ
BS 01: ¼yd (23cm) or 1FQ
BS 11: ¼yd (23cm) or 1FQ
AS 21: ¼yd (23cm) or 1FQ
GP 01-G: ⅓yd (30cm) or 1FQ
Backing fabric:
OS 01: 1½yds (1.4m)
Binding fabric:
NS 16: ½yd (45cm)

PATCH SHAPES

The centre blocks of this tablecloth are made from one small square (template BB), 1 small triangle (template KK) and 1 medium triangle (template LL). The outer border is made from 1 large triangle (template MM) see pages 78 & 81.

Templates

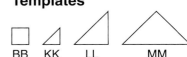

BB   KK   LL   MM

Tablecloth assembly

key

quilt centre

☐ = GP 01-G	☐ = OS 05		
☐ = OS 01	☐ = ES 20		
☐ = OS 02	☐ = NS 13		
☐ = OS 04	☐ = NS 01		
☐ = PS 04	☐ = NS 16		
☐ = BS 11	☐ = PS 22		
☐ = AS 21			
☐ = BS 01			

border horizontal stripes

☐ = OS 01	☐ = OS 02
☐ = OS 04	☐ = OS 05

border vertical stripes

☐ = ES 20	☐ = NS 01
☐ = NS 13	☐ = PS 04
☐ = BS 11	☐ = BS 01
☐ = AS 21	

CUTTING OUT

Centre blocks:

Template BB: Cut 2½in- (6.5cm-) wide strips across width of fabric. Each strip will give you 18 patches per 45in- (114cm-) wide fabric, or 9 per FQ (see page 69). Cut 64 in GP 01-G.

Template KK: Cut 3in- (7.5cm-) wide strips across width of fabric. Each strip will give you 30 patches per 45in- (114cm-) wide fabric, or 14 per FQ. Cut 28 in OS 01. Cut 32 in OS 05. Cut 34 in OS 02 and OS 04.

Template LL: Cut 5in- (12.5cm-) wide strips across width of fabric. Each strip will give you 18 patches per 45in- (114cm-) wide fabric, or 8 per FQ. Cut 4 in PS 22 and BS 01. Cut 6 in PS 04. Cut 7 in NS 01. Cut 8 in AS 21 and NS 16. Cut 9 in ES 20, NS 13 and BS 11.

Border triangles:

Horizontal stripes:

Cut 4 in OS 01. Cut 5 in OS 04 and OS 05. Cut 6 in OS 02.

Vertical stripes: Cut 1 in BS 01. Cut 2 in NS 01, NS 13 and BS 11. Cut 3 in ES 20, PS 04 and AS 21.

Straight cut binding:

Cut 4 strips 2½in- (6.5cm-) wide x width of fabric in NS 16, to form 4⅔yds (4.3m) of binding.

Backing:

Cut 1 piece 40½in x 40½in (103cm x 103cm) in OS 01.

MAKING THE BLOCKS

Using a ¼in (6mm) seam allowance, make up 64 centre blocks, following the block assembly diagrams. Make sure that you place the stripes on the top small triangles parallel to the sides of the squares, and the lower ones with the stripes at 90 degrees. This will ensure that the stripes on both small triangles will lie at right angles to the stripes on the medium triangles.

Block assembly

a   b   c

ASSEMBLING THE BLOCKS

Arrange the centre blocks into 8 rows of 8 blocks, following the tablecloth assembly diagram. Using a ¼in (6mm) seam allowance, join the blocks together in rows, then join the rows together to form the tablecloth centre.

ASSEMBLING THE BORDER

Arrange the border triangles into 4 rows of 7 patches following the quilt assembly diagram. Using a ¼in (6mm) seam allowance, join the patches to form 4 separate border strips. Attach the borders to the sides of the patchwork top. Arrange the 2 patches for each of the 4 corners. Join the patches together and attach to the corners of the tablecloth.

FINISHING THE TABLECLOTH

Press the assembled tablecloth top. Layer the top and backing, and baste together (see page 71). Attach binding to edges (see page 71).

Pale Over Under Quilt

KAFFE FASSETT

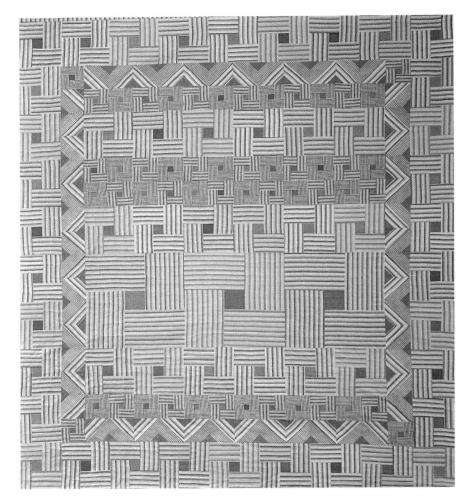

T his quilt is the same construction as the Dark Over Under Quilt (see page 44), and demonstrates extremely well how changing the colourways can create a completely different effect. This paler version evokes childhood memories of striped sundresses, beach shoes and faded deck chairs in the summer sun.

SIZE OF QUILT

The finished quilt will measure approx. 90in x 100in (228cm x 254cm).

MATERIALS

Patchwork fabrics:
OS 01: see backing fabric
OS 02: 2yds (1.8m) or 8FQ
OS 04: 1½yd (1.4m) or 7FQ
OS 05: 1½yd (1.4m) or 7FQ
BWS 01: 1¾yds (1.6m) or 7FQ
BWS 02: ¾yd (70cm) or 3FQ
SC 05: ⅛yd (15cm) or 1FQ
SC 11: ¼yd (23cm) or 1FQ
SC 14: ¼yd (23cm) or 1FQ
SC 17: ½yd (45cm) or 2FQ
SC 26: ⅛yd (15cm) or 1FQ
Backing fabric:
OS 01: 9yds (8.2m)
Binding fabric:
OS 01: see backing fabric
Batting:
98in x 108in (250cm x 275cm)
Quilting threads:
Various colours of machine quilting threads, to match fabrics.

PATCH SHAPES

The quilt top is made from 3 different sized blocks and an inner border block. Block A is formed with 4 large rectangles cut 8½in x 12½in (21.5cm x 32cm) and 1 large square (template L).
Block B is made from 4 medium rectangles (template M) and 1 medium square (template N).
Block C is made from 4 small rectangles (template O) and 1 small square (template P). The inner border blocks are made from 2 trapezoids (template Q) and 2 triangles (template R). See pages 78 & 79 for templates.

Templates

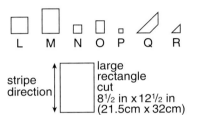

CUTTING OUT

Block A:
8½in x 12½in (21.5cm x 32cm) rectangles: Cut 4 in OS 01, OS 04, and OS 05.
Template L: Cut 1 in SC 11, SC 14 and SC 17.
Block B:
Template M: Cut 6½in- (16.5cm-) wide strips across width of fabric. Each strip will give you 9 patches per 45in- (114cm-) wide fabric, or 4 per FQ (see page 69). Cut 44 in OS 02, 52 in OS 04, and 56 in OS 01 and OS 05.
Template N: Cut 9 in SC 17, 10 in SC 14 and SC 26, 11 in SC 05, and 12 in SC 11.
Block C:
Template O: Cut 3½in- (9cm-) wide strips across width of fabric. Each strip will give you 17 patches per 45in- (114cm-) wide fabric, or 8 per FQ. Cut 104 in BWS 01 and BWS 02.
Template P: Cut 9 in SC 05, SC 17 and SC 26, 12 in SC 11, and 13 in SC 14.
Inner border blocks:
Template Q: Cut 8¼in- (21cm-) wide strips across width of fabric. Each strip will give you 16 patches per 45in- (114cm-) wide fabric, or 8 per FQ. Cut 52 in OS 02 and BWS 01.
Template R: Cut 104 in SC 17.

Quilt assembly

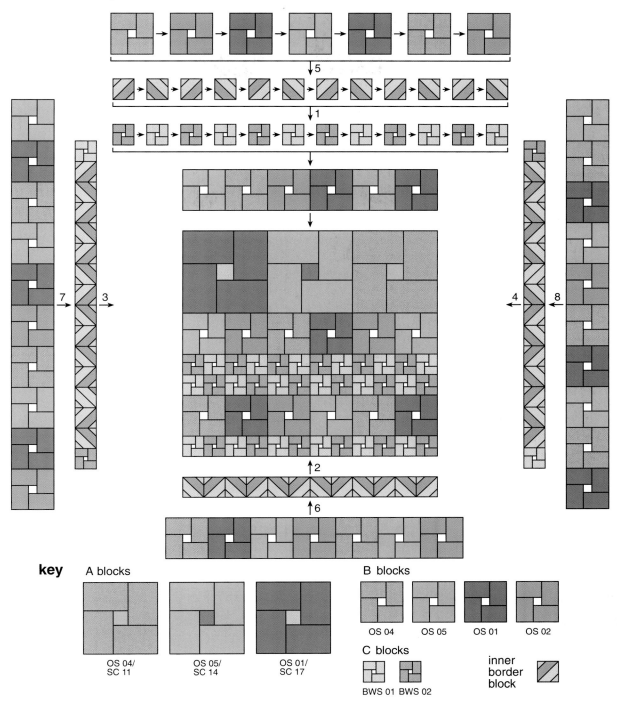

key

A blocks

OS 04/
SC 11

OS 05/
SC 14

OS 01/
SC 17

B blocks

OS 04   OS 05   OS 01   OS 02

C blocks

BWS 01   BWS 02

inner
border
block

Straight grain binding:
Cut 9 strips 2½in- (6.5cm-) wide x width of fabric in OS 01, to form 10¾yd (9.7m) of binding.

Backing:
Cut 2 pieces 45in x 98in (114cm x 250cm), and 2 pieces 19in x 49½in (48cm x 126cm) in OS 01.

MAKING THE BLOCKS
See this section in the Dark Over Under Quilt (page 45).

ASSEMBLING THE BLOCKS
Arrange the centre blocks into 8 rows of 12 C blocks, 6 B blocks, 3 A blocks, 6 B blocks, 12 C blocks, 12 C blocks,

6 B blocks and 12 C blocks following the quilt assembly diagram. Using a ¼in (6mm) seam allowance, join the blocks together into rows, then join the rows together to form the quilt centre.

For the end inner borders, arrange 2 rows of 12 inner border blocks following the quilt assembly diagram. For the side inner borders, arrange 2 rows of 14 inner border blocks, with 1 C block at each end. Join blocks together into the rows, then attach the end borders followed by the side borders. Following the quilt assembly diagram, arrange 2 rows of 7 B blocks to fit the ends of the quilt and 2 rows of 10 B blocks for the sides. Using a ¼in (6mm) seam allowance, join blocks

together into rows, then attach them to the ends first, followed by the sides.

FINISHING THE QUILT
Press the assembled quilt top. Seam the backing pieces together with a ⅜in (1cm) seam allowance to form 1 piece 98in x 108in (249 x 275cm). Layer the quilt top, batting and backing, and baste together (see page 71).

Quilt each block following the quilting diagrams on page 46. Stitch-in-the-ditch diagonally across the centre of each inner border block, forming a zigzag line of quilting.

Trim the quilt edges and attach the binding (see page 72).

Baby Pyramids Quilt

KAFFE FASSETT

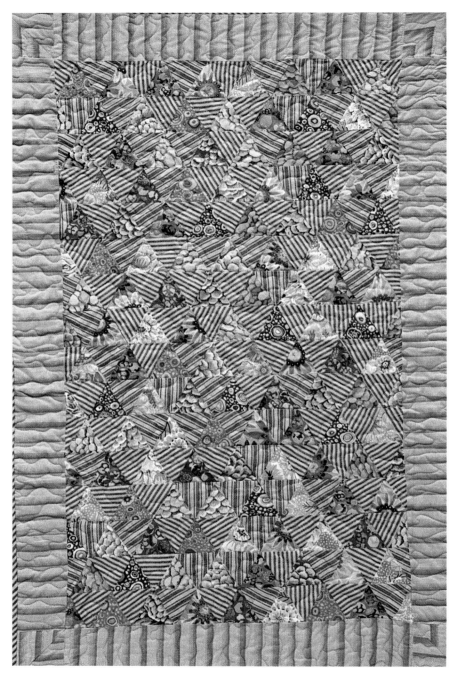

T housand Pyramids is a traditional American quilt pattern. It is a 'One patch' design, which means it is made from a single patch shape that is repeated many times. Although this quilt appears quite simple, most of the patch edges are cut on the bias, and need careful handling to avoid stretching. Alternatively, it lends itself perfectly to being made by hand using the 'English paper piecing' technique (see page 70).

SIZE OF QUILT
The finished quilt will measure approx. 42in x 26in (106cm x 66cm).

MATERIALS
Patchwork fabrics:
BWS 01: see binding fabric
BWS 02: $\frac{1}{3}$yd (30cm) or 1FQ
GP 01-G: $\frac{1}{8}$yd (15cm) or 1FQ
GP 01-S: $\frac{1}{8}$yd (15cm) or 1FQ
GP 02-P: $\frac{1}{8}$yd (15cm) or 1FQ
GP 02-S: $\frac{1}{8}$yd (15cm) or 1FQ
GP 02-C: $\frac{1}{8}$yd (15cm) or 1FQ
GP 03-S: $\frac{1}{8}$yd (15cm) or 1FQ
GP 04-J: $\frac{1}{8}$yd (15cm) or 1FQ
GP 04-S: $\frac{1}{8}$yd (15cm) or 1FQ
GP 06-J: $\frac{1}{8}$yd (15cm) or 1FQ
GP 06-S: $\frac{1}{8}$yd (15cm) or 1FQ
GP 07-P: $\frac{1}{8}$yd (15cm) or 1FQ
GP 07-S: $\frac{1}{8}$yd (15cm) or 1FQ
GP 07-L: $\frac{1}{8}$yd (15cm) or 1FQ
Border fabric:
OS 05: see backing fabric
Backing fabric:
OS 05: $1\frac{2}{3}$yd (1.6m)
Binding fabric:
BWS 01: 1yd (90cm)
Batting:
32in x 48in (81cm x 122cm)
Quilting thread:
Toning coloured machine quilting thread

PATCH SHAPES
The quilt centre is made basically from 1 patch shape: an isosceles triangle (template NN). The side edges are filled with small right angled triangles (template 00), and the border corners are made from 1 larger triangle (template PP). See pages 80 & 81 for templates.

Templates

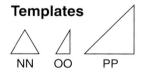

NN   OO   PP

CUTTING OUT
Template NN: Cut strips 3½in- (9cm-) wide across width of fabric. Each strip will give you 23 patches per 45in- (114cm-) wide fabric, or 11 per FQ (see page 69). Cut 5 in GP 07-L. Cut 6 in GP 02-S and GP 07-S. Cut 7 in GP 06-J. Cut 8 in GP 07-P and GP 02-C. Cut 9 in GP 04-J and GP 02-P.

Quilt assembly

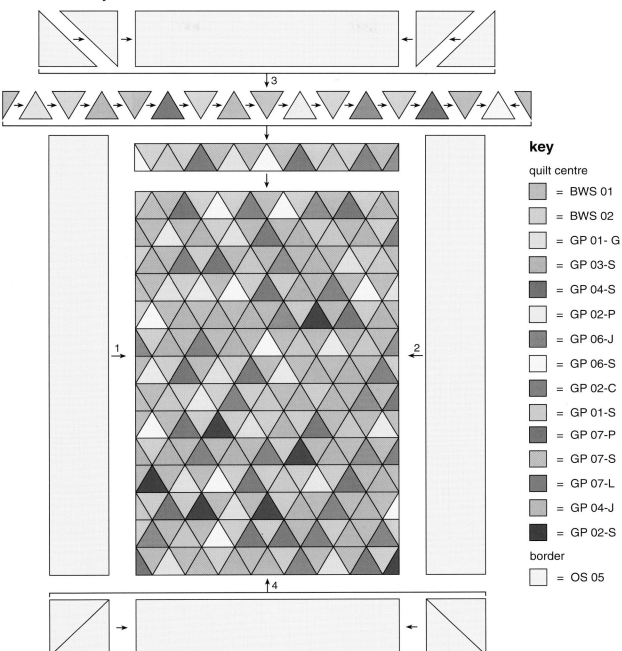

key

quilt centre

☐ = BWS 01

☐ = BWS 02

☐ = GP 01- G

☐ = GP 03-S

☐ = GP 04-S

☐ = GP 02-P

☐ = GP 06-J

☐ = GP 06-S

☐ = GP 02-C

☐ = GP 01-S

☐ = GP 07-P

☐ = GP 07-S

☐ = GP 07-L

☐ = GP 04-J

☐ = GP 02-S

border

☐ = OS 05

Cut 11 in GP 06-S and GP 01-G. Cut 12 in GP 01-S and GP 04-S. Cut 16 in GP 03-S. Cut 48 in BWS 02, and 72 in BWS 01, cutting half of each quantity with stripes horizontally and half vertically.

Template OO: Cut 4 and 6 with template reversed in BWS 01. Cut 4 and 2 with template reversed in BWS 02. Cut 1 and 2 with template reversed in GP 06-J. Cut 1 and 1 with template reversed in GP 06-S. Cut 1 in GP 01-S, and GP 04-S. Cut 2 in GP 07-S and GP 03-S. Cut 1 with template reversed in GP 01-G, GP 02-C, GP 02-S, GP 07-L and GP 07-P.

Template PP: Cut 4 and 4 with template reversed in OS 05.

Borders:

Cut 2 end border strips 3½in x 20½in (9cm x 52cm), and 2 side border strips 3½in x 36½in (9cm x 92.5cm) in OS 05, across width of fabric.

Bias binding:

Cut 4yds (3.6m) of 2½in- (6.5cm-) wide bias binding in BWS 01.

Backing:

Cut 1 piece 32in x 48in (81cm x 122cm) in OS 05, with stripes running down the length.

ASSEMBLING THE QUILT CENTRE

Following the quilt assembly diagram for fabric placement, arrange the 240 isosceles triangles into 16 rows of 15 patches, placing a right angled triangle, and a reversed right angled triangle at each end of the rows. Using a ¼in (6mm) seam allowance, and handling with great care so as not to stretch the sides, join the patches into rows, and then join the rows together to form the quilt centre.

Border corner block assembly

stripe directions

MAKING THE BORDERS

Following the border corner block assembly diagram, join a large triangle and reverse large triangle together, so that the stripes chevron down the centre seam. Using a ¼in (6mm) seam allowance, join a corner block to each end of the end border strips, making sure the corner blocks chevron outwards. Attach the 2 side borders to the edges of the quilt centre, easing in the centre if necessary. Attach the 2 end borders in the same way.

FINISHING THE QUILT

Press the assembled quilt top carefully, making sure that you don't stretch and balloon the centre out. Layer the quilt top, batting and backing, and baste together (see page 71).

Free-motion quilt the quilt centre in a very random fashion working across three rows at a time. Repeat down the whole of the quilt centre.

Using the quilting diagram as a guide, free-motion quilt in 1 long wavy row around the borders.

Trim the quilt edges and attach the binding (see page 72).

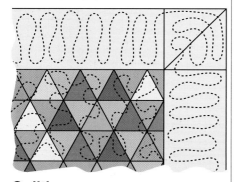

Quilting

African Stripe Baby Quilt

★

KAFFE FASSETT

Kaffe's inspiration came from African Ashanti weaving, which originated in Ghana in the 17th and 18th centuries. By placing the striped fabrics alternately vertical and horizontal, it creates the appearance of weaving the fabrics one under the other.

SIZE OF QUILT
The finished quilt will measure approx. 23in x 32in (58cm x 81cm).

MATERIALS
Patchwork fabrics:
BWS 01: see backing fabric
BWS 02: ¼yd (23cm) or 1FQ
OS 01: ⅛yd (15cm) or 1FQ
OS 02: ¼yd (23cm) or 1FQ
OS 05: ⅛yd (15cm) or 1FQ
NS 16: ⅛yd (15cm) or 1FQ
PS 04: ⅛yd (15cm) or 1FQ
AS 21: ⅛yd (15cm) or 1FQ
BC 01: ⅛yd (15cm) or 1FQ
Backing fabric:
BWS 01: 1yd (90cm)
Binding fabrics:
SC 24: ¼yd (23cm) or 1FQ
SC 27: ¼yd (23cm) or 1FQ
Batting:
27in x 35in (70cm x 89cm)

Quilt assembly

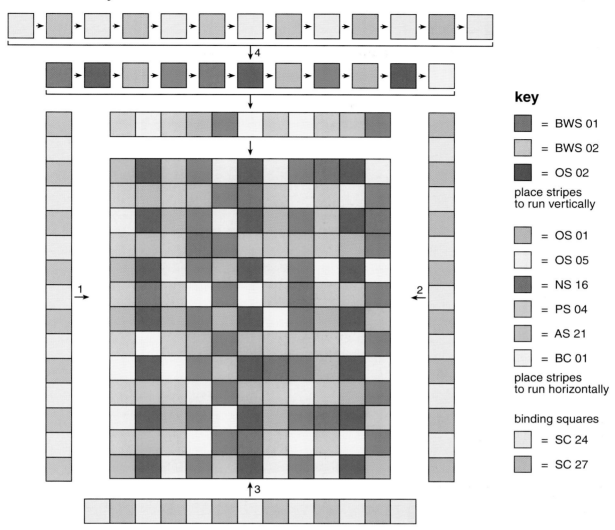

key

- = BWS 01
- = BWS 02
- = OS 02

place stripes
to run vertically

- = OS 01
- = OS 05
- = NS 16
- = PS 04
- = AS 21
- = BC 01

place stripes
to run horizontally

binding squares

- = SC 24
- = SC 27

Quilting thread:
A toning coloured machine quilting thread

PATCH SHAPES
This quilt is made from a small square, template BB. See page 78 for template.

Template

BB

CUTTING OUT
Vertical stripes:
Template BB: Cut 2½in- (6.5cm-) wide strips across width of fabric. Each strip will give you 18 patches per 45in- (114cm-) wide fabric, or 9 per FQ (see page 69). Cut 24 in OS 02, 28 in BWS 02 and 30 in BWS 01.

Horizontal stripes:
Template BB: Cut 10 in PS 04, 11 in NS 16, 12 in AS 21, 15 in BC 01, 17 in OS 01 and 18 in OS 05.
Binding squares:
Template BB: Cut 28 in SC 24 and SC 27.
Backing:
Cut 1 piece 27in x 35in (70cm x 89cm) in BWS 01, with stripes running horizontally.

ASSEMBLING QUILT TOP
Arrange the 165 squares into 15 rows of 11 patches, following the quilt assembly diagram for both colour and stripe positioning. Using a ¼in (6mm) seam allowance, join the patches into rows, then join the rows to form the quilt top.

ASSEMBLING THE BINDING
Arrange 2 rows of 15 patches for the side binding strips and 2 rows of 13 patches

for the end binding strips, using the quilt assembly diagram as a guide. Using a ¼in (6mm) seam allowance, join the patches into the 4 separate rows.

FINISHING THE QUILT
Press the assembled quilt top and binding strips. Layer the quilt top, batting and backing, and baste together (see page 71). Using a toning thread, stitch-in-the-ditch around every patch shape (see page 71). Trim quilt edges evenly, leaving approximately ¾in (2cm) of batting showing around edges of quilt top. Using the patchwork binding strips, bind each edge separately following the quilt assembly diagram, and making sure the quilt top raw edges are totally enclosed by the binding (see page 72). When attaching the top and base bindings, tuck under the raw ends at each corner and slipstitch edges together.

Grey Columns Quilt

KAFFE FASSETT

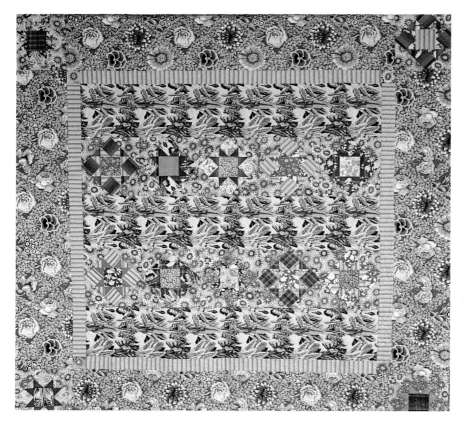

Quilting thread:
Toning coloured machine quilting thread.

PATCH SHAPES
The block used in this quilt is formed by a medium square (template QQ), a small triangle (template RR), a small square (template SS) and a large triangle (template TT). See pages 78 & 80 for templates.

Templates

QQ　RR　SS　TT

CUTTING OUT
Template QQ: Cut 1 in NC 01, OS 05, EC 01, GP 01-S, GP 01-BW, GP 02-C, GP 02-P, GP 03-S, GP 07-P, GP 07-C, GP 07-S, GP 09-S, PR 01, PR 07 and SC 27.
Template RR: Cut 4 in GP 01-S, GP 01-BW, GP 02-S, GP 02-P and GP 02-C. Cut 8 in SC 14, SC 27, EC 01, GP 07-P and GP 09-S. Cut 12 in OS 02, OS 05 and NC 01. Cut 20 in PR 01 and PR 07. Cut 32 in ES 15.
Template SS: Cut 4 in OS 02, OS 05, PR 01, PR 07, NC 01, GP 01-S, GP 01-BW, GP 02-P, GP 02-S and GP 02-C. Cut 8 in ES 15 and GP 09-S. Fussy cut 4 in GP 03-S.
Template TT: Cut 56 in GP 03-S.
Straight bands:
Cut 3 pieces 68in x 14in (172cm x 35.5cm) in GP 09-S.
Inner borders:
Cut 8 strips across width of fabric 34¼in x 3⅝in (87cm x 9cm) in OS 05.
Outer borders:
Cut 8 rectangles 37½in x 14in (95cm x 35.5cm) in GP 11-S, centralizing the floral design, and matching up the pattern repeats across each pair.
Straight cut binding:
Cut 10 strips 2½in- (6.5cm-) wide x width of fabric in ES 04, to form 11⅓yds (10.3m) of binding.
Backing:
Cut 2 pieces 45in x 108in (114cm x

T
his quilt is a larger version of the Red Columns Quilt (see page 56). It is quite heavily quilted, but much more loosely than the Red version, by following the fabric print designs, or using simple free-motion quilting. The only areas to use a template are the inner borders, which you can choose to omit if you wish.

SIZE OF QUILT
The finished quilt will measure approx.imately 100in x 100in (254cm x 254cm).

MATERIALS
Patchwork fabrics:
GP 01-BW: ¼yd (23cm) or 1FQ
GP 01-S: ¼yd (23cm) or 1FQ
GP 02-P: ¼yd (23cm) or 1FQ
GP 02-C: ¼yd (23cm) or 1FQ
GP 02-S: ⅛yd (15cm) or 1FQ
GP 03-S: 1½yds (1.3m) or 6FQ
GP 07-S: ¼yd (23cm) or 1FQ
GP 07-P: ¼yd (23cm) or 1FQ
GP 07-C: ¼yd (23cm) or 1FQ
GP 09-S: See straight band fabric
PR 01: ¼yd (23cm) or 1FQ
PR 07: ⅓yd (30cm) or 1FQ

NC 01: ¼yd (23cm) or 1FQ
EC 01: ¼yd (23cm) or 1FQ
OS 02: ⅛yd (15cm) or 1FQ
OS 05: see backing fabric
ES 15: ¼yd (23cm) or 1FQ
SC 14: ⅛yd (15cm) or 1FQ
SC 27: ¼yd (23cm) or 1FQ
Straight band fabric:
GP 09-S: 2⅓yds (2.1m)
Inner border fabric:
OS 05: see backing fabric
Outer border fabric:
GP 11-S: 3⅓yds (3.1m)
Backing fabric:
OS 05: 8½yds (7.8m)
Binding fabric:
ES 04: ¾yd (70cm)
Batting:
108in x 108in (275cm x 275cm)

Quilt assembly

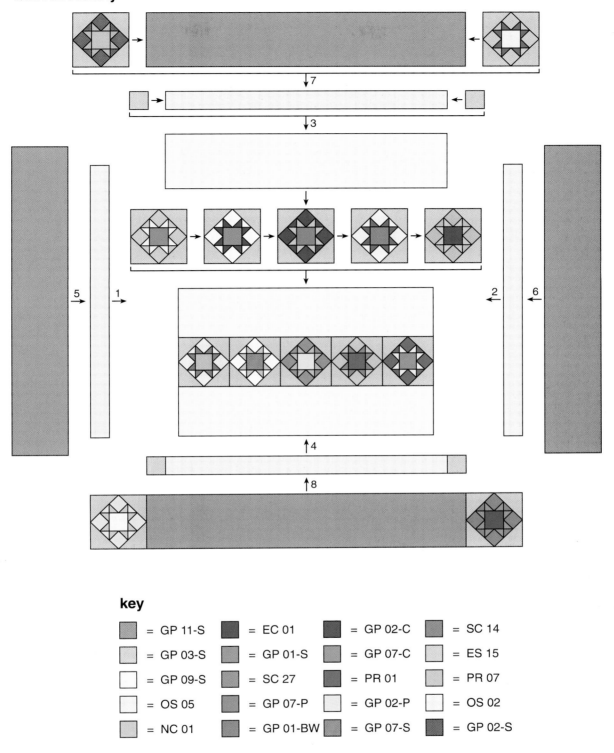

key

= GP 11-S		= EC 01		= GP 02-C		= SC 14	
= GP 03-S		= GP 01-S		= GP 07-C		= ES 15	
= GP 09-S		= SC 27		= PR 01		= PR 07	
= OS 05		= GP 07-P		= GP 02-P		= OS 02	
= NC 01		= GP 01-BW		= GP 07-S		= GP 02-S	

274cm), and 2 pieces 19½in x 54½in (49.5cm x 138.5cm) in OS 05.

MAKING THE BLOCKS

Using a ¼in (6mm) seam allowance, make up 14 blocks following the block assembly diagrams in the Red Columns Quilt, see page 57, and the Grey Columns Quilt assembly diagram as a fabric guide.

ASSEMBLING THE QUILT CENTRE

Arrange 2 rows of 5 blocks in between the 3 straight bands, following the quilt assembly diagram.

Using a ¼in (6mm) seam allowance, join the blocks together into 2 rows, then join the rows to the straight bands to form the centre of the quilt top.

MAKING INNER BORDERS

Join the inner border strips to form 4 pieces 68in x 3⅝in (172cm x 9cm). Attach a fussy cut square (template QQ) to each end of 2 strips to form the end borders, see quilt assembly diagram. Attach the 2 side borders (without the squares) to the edges of the quilt, and then the end borders.

55

MAKING THE OUTER BORDERS

Using a ¼in (6mm) seam allowance, join the rectangles together in pairs, matching up the pattern repeats, to form 4 bands 74¼in x 14in (188.5cm x 35.5cm). Attach 1 of the remaining blocks to each end of 2 borders to form the end borders (see quilt assembly diagram).

Attach the 2 side borders (without the blocks) to the edges of the quilt, and then the end borders.

PREPARING THE QUILT FOR QUILTING

Press the assembled quilt top. Seam the backing pieces together to form one piece measuring approximately 108in x 108in (275cm x 275cm). Layer the quilt top, batting and backing, and baste together (see page 71).

QUILTING AND FINISHING THE QUILT

On the centre square of each block, and the inner border squares, loosely stitch following the print design on the fabric. Using the quilting diagram below, as a guide, free-motion quilt the 4 large triangles, 4 small triangles and 4 squares of each block.

On the straight bands, loosely quilt following the leaves on the chard print design.

Stitch-in-the-ditch around each border and around each patch shape in the borders.

Using the inner border leaf template (see page 86), transfer the motifs, repeating it along the length of each inner border. Stitch design in place.

Finally, to quilt the outer borders, loosely stitch around each flower shape on the fabric.

Trim the quilt edges and attach the binding (see page 72).

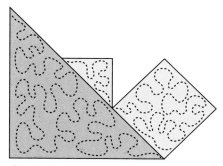

Quilting

Red Columns Quilt ★★★

KAFFE FASSETT

This project has 3 stars because of its heavy quilting, but don't be daunted by this. Basically, the centre of each star block has a daisy motif and the borders are quilted by loosely following the flower petals printed on the fabric, with a daisy motif in between. As an alternative, simply stitch-in-the-ditch around each patch shape and free-motion quilt the borders.

SIZE OF QUILT

The finished quilt will measure approx. 68in x 68in (172cm x 172cm).

MATERIALS

Patchwork fabrics:
GP 01-R: ¼yd (23cm) or 1FQ
GP 01-G: 1yd (90cm) or 4FQ
GP 02-J: ¼yd (23cm) or 1FQ
GP 07-J: ¼yd (23cm) or 1FQ
GP 08-J: ¼yd (23cm) or 1FQ
AS 03: ¼yd (23cm) or 1FQ
AS 10: ¼yd (23cm) or 1FQ
AS 21: ¼yd (23cm) or 1FQ
PS 13: ¼yd (23cm) or 1FQ
NC 03: ¼yd (23cm) or 1FQ
BS 01: see binding fabric
PR 04: ¼yd (23cm) or 1FQ
PR 06: ¼yd (23cm) or 1FQ
NS 17: ¼yd (23cm) or 1FQ
SC 09: ⅛yd (15cm) or 1FQ
ES 15: ⅛yd (15cm) or 1FQ
Straight band fabric:
GP 11-C: 2½yds (2.3m)

Quilt assembly

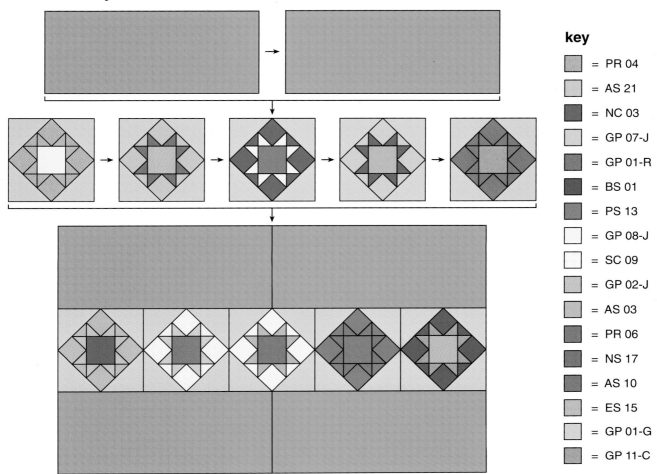

key

- = PR 04
- = AS 21
- = NC 03
- = GP 07-J
- = GP 01-R
- = BS 01
- = PS 13
- = GP 08-J
- = SC 09
- = GP 02-J
- = AS 03
- = PR 06
- = NS 17
- = AS 10
- = ES 15
- = GP 01-G
- = GP 11-C

Backing fabric:
NS 16: 4yds (3.7m)
Binding fabric:
BS 01: ⅔yd (60cm) or 2FQ
Batting:
72in x 72in (183cm x 183cm)
Quilting thread:
Claret coloured machine quilting thread

PATCH SHAPES

The block used in this quilt is formed by a medium square (template QQ), a small triangle (template RR), a small square (template SS) and a large triangle (template TT). See pages 78 & 80 for templates.

Templates

QQ   RR   SS   TT

CUTTING OUT

Template QQ: Cut 1 in GP 08-J, PS 13, AS 03, AS 10, PR 04, PR 06, NS 17 and NC 03. Cut 2 in GP 02-J.
Template RR: Cut 4 in BS 01 and SC 09. Cut 8 in ES 15, NS 17 and AS 03. Cut 12 in GP 01-R, GP 07-J, GP 08-J, NC 03, AS 21, PR 04 and PS 13.
Template SS: Cut 4 in PR 04, AS 21, NC 03, BS 01, SC 09, PS 13, GP 07-J and GP 08-J.
Template TT: Cut 40 in GP 01-G.
Straight bands:
Cut 6 rectangles 34¼in x 14in (87cm x 35.5cm) in GP 11-C, centralizing the floral design and matching up the pattern repeats across each pair.
Bias binding:
Cut 7¾yds (7.1m) of 2½in- (6.5cm-) wide bias binding in BS 01.
Backing:
Cut 2 pieces 72in x 36in (183cm x 91cm) in NS 16.

MAKING THE BLOCKS

Using a ¼in (6mm) seam allowance, make up 10 blocks following the block assembly diagrams and quilt assembly diagram as a fabric guide.

Block assembly

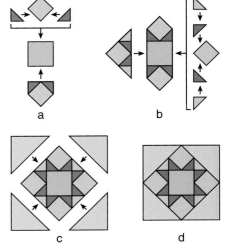

MAKING THE STRAIGHT BANDS

Using a ¼in (6mm) seam allowance, join the rectangles together in pairs, matching up the pattern repeats, to form 3 strips 68in x 14in (173cm x 35.5).

ASSEMBLING QUILT TOP

Arrange 2 rows of 5 blocks in between the 3 straight bands, following the quilt assembly diagram (previous page). Using a ¼in (6mm) seam allowance, join the blocks together into 2 rows, then join rows to straight bands to form quilt top.

PREPARING THE QUILT FOR QUILTING

Press the assembled quilt top. Seam the backing pieces together to form one piece measuring approximately 72in x 72in (183cm x 183cm). Layer the quilt top, batting and backing, and baste together (see page 71).

QUILTING AND FINISHING THE QUILT

Using the daisy motif template (see page 86), transfer the design on to the centre square of each block and stitch the daisy shape (see page 71). Using the quilting template for the large triangle (see page 86), transfer and stitch the design onto the 4 large triangles of each block. To complete the block quilting, free-motion quilt the 4 small squares and 4 small outer triangles using the block quilting diagram as a guide below. To quilt the straight bands, loosely stitch around each flower shape on the fabric. Using the daisy template and straight band quilting diagram below as a guide, stitch a daisy at the crossroads between the flowers, and freehand stitch stems and leaves to join the daisies together. Trim the quilt edges and attach the binding (see page 72).

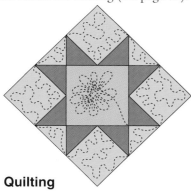

Quilting

Straight bands quilting

Amish Star Quilt ★★

LIZA PRIOR LUCY

This quilt is an interpretation of an traditional Amish quilt from Pennsylvania. Amish quilts were made of fabric scraps, and often colours were mismatched. The shot cotton fabrics make this look easy to achieve, as the fabric is woven with different coloured warp and weft yarns. This makes the fabric appear a slightly different colour when turned through ninety degrees.

SIZE OF QUILT

The finished quilt will measure approximately 72in x 72in (183cm x 183cm).

MATERIALS

Patchwork fabrics:
SC 05: ½yd (45cm) or 2FQ
SC 10: ¾yd (70m) or 5FQ
SC 11: ¼yd (23cm) or 1FQ
SC 12: ½yd (45cm) or 2FQ
SC 14: ½yd (45cm) or 2FQ
SC 18: 1⅛yd (1m) or 4FQ
Outer borders and binding fabric:
SC 03: 2¾yds (2.5m)

Backing fabric:
PS 08: 4½yds (4.1m)
Batting:
80in x 80in (2m x 2m)
Quilting thread:
Black Perle cotton, or fine crochet cotton.

PATCH SHAPES

The quilt top is made from 3 different blocks. Block A is formed with 1 large square cut 12½in x 12½in (32cm x 32cm), 4 medium sized squares (template T), and 16 medium triangles (template S).
Block B is formed by 1 medium square (template T), 4 small squares (template V)

Quilt assembly

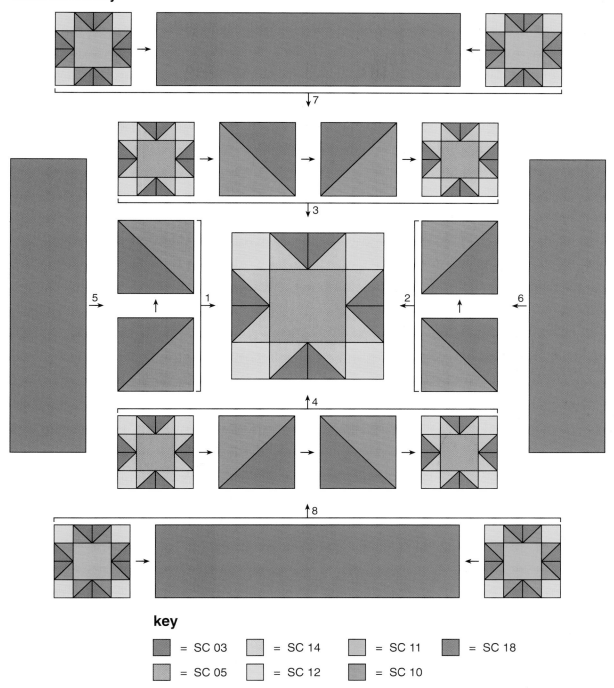

key

■ = SC 03	☐ = SC 14	■ = SC 11	■ = SC 18
■ = SC 05	☐ = SC 12	■ = SC 10	

and 16 small triangles (template U). See pages 81, 82 & 83 for templates.

Templates

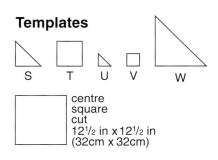

S T U V W

centre square
cut
12½ in x 12½ in
(32cm x 32cm)

Block C is made from 2 large triangles (template W). You find 2 quarters of this triangle on page 83. Copy off the 2 pieces and overlap the shaded areas. Stick together to form a half template. Place fold edge of template to fold of paper and trace around the shape. Cut out double thickness, and open out for a complete template W.

CUTTING OUT
Block A:
Cut 1 square 12½in x 12½in (32cm x 32cm) in SC 05.
Template S: Cut 8 in SC 18 and SC 14.
Template T: Cut 4 in SC 12.

Block B:
Template T: Cut 4 in SC 05 and SC 11.
Template U: Cut 32 in SC 14 and SC 10, and 64 in SC 18.
Template V: Cut 32 in SC 12.
Block C:
Template W: Cut 8 in SC 10 and SC 18.
Borders:
Cut 4 pieces 12½in x 48½in (32cm x 124cm) in SC 03.
Straight grain binding:
Cut 8¼yds x 2¼in (7.55m x 6cm) of binding from the remainder of SC 03.
Backing:
Cut 2 pieces 40½in x 80in (103cm x 203cm) in PS 08.

MAKING THE BLOCKS

Following the block assembly diagrams, and using the quilt assembly diagram (previous page) as a colour guide, make up 1 A block and 4 B blocks in the same colourways, 4 B blocks in the second colourway and 8 C blocks, using a ¼in (6mm) seam allowance.

Blocks A and B assembly

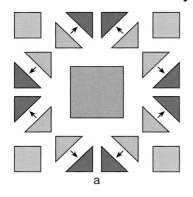

a

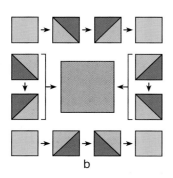

b

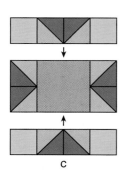

c

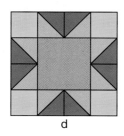

d

Block C assembly

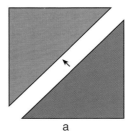

a

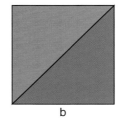

b

ASSEMBLING THE BLOCKS

Following the quilt assembly diagram (previous page), join 2 C blocks to form a point at the centre. Repeat with 2 more C blocks, and join these to each side of Block A, with the points facing inwards. Arrange 2 rows of 2 C blocks (forming a point at the centre), with a B block at each end coloured the same as Block A. Join blocks together into 2 rows. Join a row to the opposite sides of block A, with the C blocks pointing inwards.

Stitch a border to 2 opposite sides of the quilt top. Arrange the remaining 2 borders with a differently coloured B block at each end. Join the blocks to the border ends and join the borders to the remaining 2 sides of the quilt top.

FINISHING THE QUILT

Press the assembled quilt top. Seam the backing pieces together with a ⅜in (1cm) seam allowance, to form 1 piece 80in x 80in (203cm x 203cm). Layer the quilt top, batting and backing, and baste together (see page 71).

Block A: Using a 6in (15cm) plate as a template, mark a circle in the centre of the block, and lines that radiate out from the circle to bisect each triangle and square (see quilting diagram right for a guide). Work large evenly spaced hand-quilting stitches (see page 71) around the circle and along the lines.

Block B: Mark and work a 4in (10cm) circle in each of the centre squares.

Block C: Using the quilting diagram as a guide, mark a semi-circle with a radius of 3¼in (8cm) across 2 blocks with the seam running up the centre. Work the quilting stitches. From the semi-circle, work 2 evenly spaced straight rows of quilting radiating out to the diagonal seam, and one along the vertical seam between the two blocks. On the remaining triangle in the block, work 6 straight rows of quilting, spaced 1¼in (3cm) apart, parallel to the diagonal seam.

Borders: Enlarge the border quilting template on a photocopier until it measures 12in (30.5cm) square (see page 85). Use template to mark the wave pattern, by repeating the template 4 times along each border. Hand quilt along the lines.

Trim the quilt edges and attach the binding (see page 72).

block A

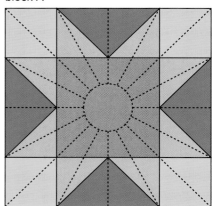

block B

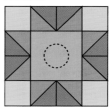

block C

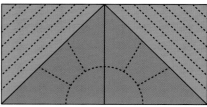

Quilting

Tote Bag

LIZA PRIOR LUCY

T his pretty and fashionable bag is made from a combination of patchwork squares and appliqué. The motifs are simply cut from printed fabric, eliminating the need for templates. It's the perfect bag, whether you're on holiday or a shopping spree.

SIZE OF BAG
The finished bag will measure approx. 24in x 16in (60cm x 40cm).

MATERIALS
Patchwork fabrics:
SC 14: ¼yd (23cm) or 1FQ
SC 16: ¼yd (23cm) or 1FQ
SC 17: ¼yd (23cm) or 1FQ
SC 19: ¼yd (23cm) or 1FQ
SC 20: ¼yd (23cm) or 1FQ
SC 21: ¼yd (23cm) or 1FQ
Appliqué fabrics:
GP 03-J: ¼yd (23cm)

GP 01-L: ¼yd (23cm)
Base fabric:
SC 22: ¼yd (23cm) or 1FQ
Lining fabric:
BS 06: 1yd (90cm)
Straps and base stiffener:
NS 01: 1yd (90cm)
Medium-weight iron-on interfacing:
1½yd (1.4m) x 36in- (90cm-) wide
Paper-backed adhesive web:
⅔yd (60cm) of 17½in- (45cm-)wide
Appliqué threads:
Assorted colours of machine thread.

Cardboard stiffener:
5¾in x 17¾in (14.5cm x 45cm) of thick stiff card.

PATCH SHAPES
The bag is formed from one patch shape: a large square (template JJ) see page 82. Place fold edge of template to fold of paper, trace around the shape and cut out double thickness to form the complete template.

CUTTING OUT
Bag sides:
Template JJ: Cut 2 in SC 14, SC 16, SC 17, SC 19, SC 20 and SC 21.
Bag base:
Cut 1 rectangle 6½in x 18½in (16.5cm x 47cm) in SC 22 and BS 06.
Lining:
Cut 2 side pieces 16½in x 24½in (42cm x 62cm) in BS 06.
Cut 1 inner base cover 13in x 20in (33cm x 51cm) in NS 01.
Straps:
Cut 3 strips 4½in-(11.5cm-) wide x the width of the fabric, in NS 01.
Appliqué shapes:
Iron the fusible web on to the reverse side of each appliqué fabric. Then, fussy cut 12 daisies from GP 03-J and 144 spots of varying sizes from GP 01-L.
Interfacing:
Template JJ: Cut 12.
Straps: Cut 3 strips 4½in x 45cm (11.5cm x 114cm).

MAKING THE BLOCKS
Iron the interfacing to the wrong side of each large square. Then, working with one square at a time, peel the paper backing from 1 daisy and place it in the centre. Arrange an assortment of 12 spots in a circle around the daisy. Iron shapes in place and appliqué around all raw edges (see page 70). Repeat for each square.

ASSEMBLING THE BLOCKS
For each side arrange 2 rows of 3 blocks using the photograph above as a guide. Using a ¼in (6mm) seam allowance, join the blocks together into rows, then join the rows to form the 2 the bag sides. Press assembled bag sides.

FINISHING OFF THE BAG
For full instructions on how to complete the bag, turn to page 72 in the Patchwork Know-how section.

Ambrosia Cushion

KIM HARGREAVES

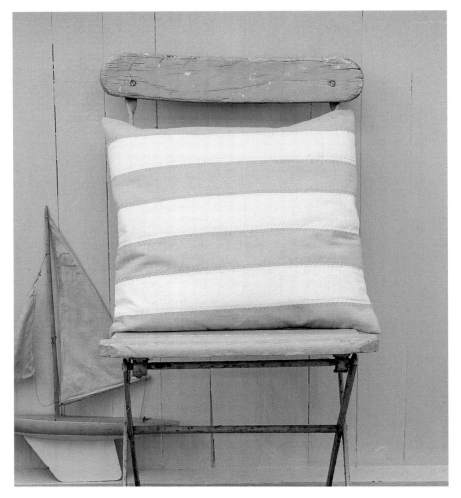

T his cushion is an ideal project for a beginner to start with. It's a very quick project that could easily be made in an evening. By changing the stripe colour combinations you can create very different looks.

SIZE OF CUSHION COVER
The finished cushion cover will measure approximately 17½in x 17½in (45cm x 45cm).

MATERIALS
Patchwork fabrics:
SC 24: ½yd (45cm) or 2FQ
SC 28: ½yd (45cm) or 1FQ
Binding fabric:
SC 24: see Patchwork fabrics
Lining:
⅔yd (60cm) x 45in- (114cm-) wide lining
Batting:
20in x 20in (50cm x 50cm)

Cushion pad:
18in x 18in (45cm x 45cm)
Quilting thread:
Matching ecru and pale pink embroidery thread, or fine crotchet cotton.

PATCH SHAPES
The front and back cover are formed with 3in- (7.5cm-) strips of contrasting fabric.

CUTTING OUT
Front cover:
Cut 4 strips 3in x 18in (7.5cm x 46cm) in SC 24.
Cut 3 strips 3in x 18in (7.5cm x 46cm) in SC 28.

Back cover:
Cut 8 strips 3in x 10½in (7.5cm x 27cm) in SC 24.
Cut 6 strips 3in x 10½in (7.5cm x 27cm) in SC 28.
Straight grain binding:
Cut 2 strips 2½in x 18in (6.5cm x 46cm) in SC 24.
Lining:
Cut 1 piece 20in x 20in (50cm x 50cm).

MAKING THE CUSHION TOP
Arrange the 7 strips alternating the colours, and using a ¼in (6mm) seam allowance, join the strips together.

MAKING THE CUSHION BACKS
Arrange 7 strips alternating the colours, and using a ¼in (6mm) seam allowance, join the strips together. Repeat with the remaining 7 strips for the second back. Press the 2 assembled backs and put to one side.

QUILTING THE TOP
Press the assembled cushion top. Layer top, batting and lining, and baste together (see page 71). Hand quilt with a row of stitching ⅛in (3mm) and ¼in (6mm) each side of the seamlines with matching thread. Trim the batting and lining edges level with the cushion top.

FINISHING OFF THE COVER
For full instructions on how to complete the cushion cover, turn to page 73 in the Patchwork Know-how section.

Hush and Lavender Cushions ★

KIM HARGREAVES

QUILTING THE HUSH CUSHION TOP

Layer the top, batting and lining, and baste together (see page 71). Using the photograph left as a guide, mark a cross on the cushion top to divide it into 4 equal quarters. Using charcoal coloured thread, work a hand-quilted row along both lines of the cross, see page 71.

In each quarter of the cushion mark a 4in (10cm) square placed 1in (2.5cm) away from the quilted cross lines. Using the charcoal thread, work a row around each square, and then work a second row inside the squares spaced ¼in (6mm) apart. Work the first pink squares, ¾in (2cm) inside the last charcoal rows, then work 1 further square inside these, spaced ¼in (6mm) apart.

QUILTING THE LAVENDER CUSHION TOP

Layer the top, batting and lining, and baste together (see page 71). Using the photograph below as a guide, mark a 5½in (14cm) square in the centre of the cushion top (see page 71). Using the green thread, work a hand quilted row around the square. Work 3 more green rows inside the square, spaced ⅜in (1cm) apart. Work the first pink square 1in (2.5cm) inside the last green row, then work 2 further rows inside this, spaced ¼in (6mm) apart.

FINISHING OFF THE COVER

For full instructions on how to complete the cushion cover, turn to page 73 in the Patchwork Know-how section.

These cushions don't involve any patchwork – they're purely quilting projects. They're very suitable for beginners, as the quilting is done by hand in simple square shapes. Choose from the two designs, or have a go at both.

SIZE OF CUSHION COVERS

The finished cushion covers will measure approximately 17½in x 17½in (45cm x 45cm).

MATERIALS

For one cover
Cover fabric:
SC 14 or SC 23: ⅔yd (60cm)
Binding fabric:
BC 01: ¼yd (23cm) or 1FQ
Lining:
⅔yd (60cm) x 45in- (114cm-) wide lining

Batting:
20in x 20in (50cm x 50cm)
Cushion pad:
18in x 18in (45cm x 45cm)
Quilting threads:
Charcoal grey and rose pink embroidery threads, or fine crotchet cotton.

CUTTING OUT

Cut 1 front 18in x 18in (45cm x 45cm) in SC 14 or SC 23.
Cut 2 backs 10½in x 18in (26.5cm x 45cm) in SC 14 or SC 23.
Cut 2 binding strips 2½in x 18in (6.5cm x 46cm) in BC 01.

Echo Quilt

KIM HARGREAVES

★★

Backing fabric:
SC 24: 8¼yds (7.6m)
Binding fabric:
SC 23: 1¼yds (1.2m)
Batting:
70in x 95in (178cm x 241cm)
Quilting threads:
Ecru, pewter, burgundy and charcoal embroidery threads, or fine crotchet cotton
Quilters' tape:
2 reels ¼in- (6mm-) wide

PATCH SHAPES
This quilt uses one template only: a small square for the inner border corners (template V). See page 81 for template.

Template

V

CUTTING OUT
Quilt centre:
Cut 1 oblong 31½in x 55½in (80cm x 141cm) in SC 24.
Inner borders:
Cut 4 strips 3½in x 27¾in (9cm x 70.5cm) for the side borders, and 2 strips 3½in x 31½in (9cm x 80cm) for the end borders in SC 23.
Inner border corners:
Template V: Cut 4 in SC 02.
Outer borders:
Cut 2 side borders 14¼in x 61½in (36cm x 156.5cm), and 2 end borders 14¼in x 37½in (36cm x 95.5cm) in SC 24.
Outer border corners:
Cut 4 squares 14¼in x 14¼in (36cm x 36cm) in SC 25.
Straight grain binding:
Cut 7 strips 2½in- (6.5cm-) wide x width of fabric in SC 23, to form 8¾yds (7.9m) of binding.
Backing:
Cut 2 pieces 45in x 70in (114cm x 178cm), and 2 pieces 9in x 35½in (23cm x 90cm) in SC 24.

ASSEMBLING THE QUILT
Using a ¼in (6mm) seam allowance join 2 side inner border strips to make 2 strips measuring 3½in x 55½in (9cm x 141cm). Following the quilt assembly diagram opposite, attach the 2 inner side borders

P atchwork and quilting is a new venture for Kim. Well known for her knitwear designs, Kim's style is simple and uncluttered in contrast to the intricate designs of Kaffe. The inspiration for this quilt came from old Amish designs she saw on a trip to America in the 1980s. Giving them a cool, modern twist, she's produced a quilt, that's easy to construct, but whose main beauty lies in the mass of simple hand quilting that covers the entire quilt.

SIZE OF QUILT
The finished quilt will measure approx. 65in x 89in (165cm x 226cm).

MATERIALS
Patchwork fabrics
Centre rectangle:
SC 24: see backing fabric

Inner borders:
SC 23: see binding fabric
Inner border corners:
SC 02: ⅛yd (15cm) or 1FQ
Outer borders:
SC 24: see backing fabric
Outer border corners:
SC 25: 1yd (90cm)

Quilt assembly

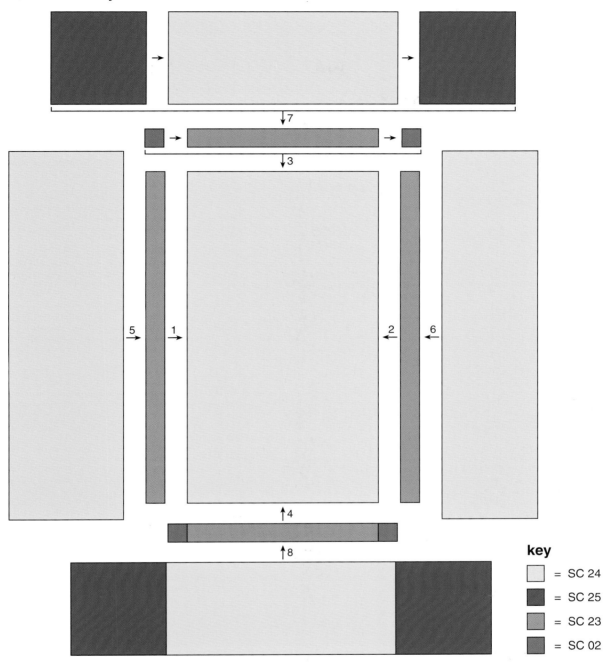

key

☐	= SC 24
■	= SC 25
▨	= SC 23
▨	= SC 02

to the edges of the quilt centre. Attach an inner border corner block to each end of the 2 inner border end strips, and attach these to the ends of the quilt centre. Join an outer border corner square to each end of the outer border end strips. Then, firstly attach the outer borders to the sides, and then the ends.

PREPARING THE QUILT FOR QUILTING

Press the assembled quilt top. Seam the backing pieces together to form one piece measuring approximately 70in x 95in (178cm x 241cm). Layer the quilt top, batting and backing, and baste together (see page 71).

Grid diagram

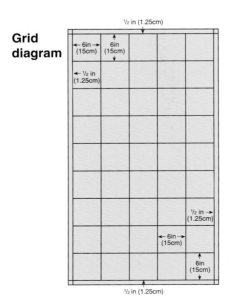

½ in (1.25cm)

← 6in → (15cm)   6in (15cm)

← ½ in (1.25cm)

½ in → (1.25cm)

← 6in → (15cm)

6in (15cm)

½ in (1.25cm)

QUILTING THE CENTRE SECTION

Using ¼in- (6mm-) wide quilters' tape, mark out a grid on the quilt centre following the grid diagram left. Working on one section at a time, mark a square in each section of the grid, 1in (2.5cm) in from the edges of the tape (see page 71). Using ecru coloured thread, work a hand-quilted row around the marked square. Work 3 further concentric rows of quilting stitches inside the first square, spaced ¼in (6mm) apart (see quilting diagram overleaf for a guide). Continue until whole centre is quilted. Do not remove adhesive tape at this point.

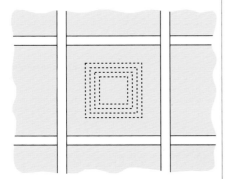

Centre squares quilting

QUILTING THE INNER BORDERS

Using the triangular quilting template (see page 84), mark a zigzag quilting line centrally along each inner border, matching the points up to the quilters' tape lines. Work the quilting row in pewter coloured thread.

For the inner border corners, mark and work 3 concentric square rows of stitching spaced ⅜in (1cm) apart in burgundy coloured thread.

QUILTING THE OUTER BORDERS AND FINISHING

Using the quilting diagram as a guide, mark the first rectangular row 1in (2.5cm) in from the seamed edges of the outer border, and 1½in (4cm) in from the outer edges of the quilt. Stitch first row in ecru coloured thread, and then mark and work 5 more concentric rectangles spaced 1in (2.5cm) apart.

For the outer border corners, mark the first row 1in (2.5cm) in from the seamed edges and 1½in (4cm) in from the quilt edges. Stitch first row in charcoal coloured thread, and then mark and work 5 more concentric squares spaced 1in (2.5cm) apart.

Trim quilt edges, and attach binding (see page 72).

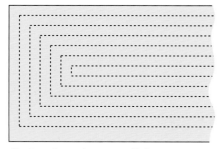

Outer borders quilting

Psychedelic Flowers

★★★

KAREN STONE

This amazing project is a combination of patchwork and appliqué. Squares of contrasting fabric form the appliqué. When cut up into the design all the pieces are used on opposing blocks, to form the positive and negative effect.

SIZE OF WALL HANGING
The finished wall hanging will measure approximately 45in x 45in (114cm x 114cm).

MATERIALS
Patchwork fabrics:
Base squares
SC 02: ⅓yd (30cm) or 1FQ
SC 03: ⅓yd (30cm) or 1FQ
SC 07: ⅓yd (30cm) or 1FQ
SC 09: ⅓yd (30cm) or 1FQ
SC 10: ⅓yd (30cm) or 1FQ
SC 13: ⅓yd (30cm) or 1FQ
SC 15: ⅓yd (30cm) or 1FQ

SC 21: ⅓yd (30cm) or 1FQ
SC 22: ⅓yd (30cm) or 1FQ
Appliqué squares
GP 01-P: ⅓yd (30cm) or 1FQ
GP 03-C: ⅓yd (30cm) or 1FQ
GP 06-C: ⅓yd (30cm) or 1FQ
GP 09-J: ⅓yd (30cm) or 1FQ
BC 04: see backing and binding fabric
SC 14: ⅓yd (30cm) or 1FQ
Border triangles
ES 15: ⅓yd (30cm) or 1FQ
ES 21: ⅓yd (30cm) or 1FQ
EC 01: ⅓yd (30cm) or 1FQ
EC 05: ⅓yd (30cm) or 1FQ
BS 06: ⅓yd (30cm) or 1FQ

Inner border fabric:
GP 01-J: ½yd (45cm)
Outer border fabric:
BS 01: ½yd (45cm)
Backing and binding fabric:
BC 04: 2yds (1.8m)
Paper-backed adhesive web:
1yd (90m) of 17½in (45cm) wide
Dressmakers' carbon paper
Appliqué threads:
Assorted colours of machine thread

PATCH SHAPES

The wall hanging centre is made from two patch shapes, 1 large square (template HH) and 1 large triangle (template II). You'll find half of each template on pages 83 & 85. Place fold edge of each template to fold of paper, trace around shape and cut out double thickness to create the complete templates. There is also an appliqué template on page 84, which needs to be enlarged on a photocopier to the same size as template HH, the large square.

Templates

HH   II   appliqué design

CUTTING OUT

Base squares:
Template HH: Cut 1 in SC 02, SC 03, SC 07, SC 09, SC 10 and SC 15. Cut 2 in SC 13, SC 21 and SC 22.
Appliqué squares:
Template HH: Cut 1 in GP 01-P, GP 03-C, GP 06-C, GP 09-J, BC 04 and SC 14. Cut 6 in paper-backed adhesive web.
Outer triangles:
Template II: Cut 2 in ES 15, ES 21, BS 06, EC 01 and EC 05.
Inner borders:
Cut 4 end border strips 2in x 36½in (5cm x 93cm), and 4 side strips 2in x 39½in (5cm x 100cm), in GP 01-J.
Outer borders:
Cut 2 end border strips across width of fabric, 3¼in x 39½in (8cm x 100cm), and 2 side strips across the width of fabric, 3¼in x 45in (8cm x 114cm), in BS 01.
Straight grain binding:
Cut 5 strips 2in- (5cm-) wide x width of fabric in BC 04, to form 5¼yds (4.8m) of binding.
Backing:
Cut 1 piece 45in x 45in (114cm x114cm) in BC 04.
Fusible web:
Template HH: Cut 6.

MAKING THE BLOCKS

Iron an adhesive web square on to the reverse side of each appliqué square, and using the dressmakers' carbon paper, transfer the appliqué design on to each paper backing. Cut out all the appliqué shapes along the design lines. Using the block assembly diagrams as a guide (below right), peel the paper backing from each numbered section of the appliqué design and position them onto the backing fabrics, following the block combinations below. Appliqué the shapes in place (see page 70).

BLOCK COMBINATIONS

Block A:
Background: SC 02
Appliqué 2: GP 03-C
Appliqué 4: SC 14
Appliqué 5: GP 06-C
Appliqué 7: BC 04
Block B:
Background: SC 22
Appliqué 1: GP 01-P
Appliqué 3: BC 04
Appliqué 6: GP 03-C
Block C:
Background: SC 07
Appliqué 1: SC 14
Appliqué 3: GP 01-P
Appliqué 6: GP 06-C
Block D:
Background: SC 21
Appliqué 2: BC 04
Appliqué 4: GP 03-C
Appliqué 5: GP 01-P
Appliqué 7: GP 09-J
Block E:
Background: SC 13
Appliqué 1: BC 04
Appliqué 3: GP 06-C
Appliqué 6: GP 01-P
Block F:
Background: SC 03
Appliqué 2: GP 09-J
Appliqué 4: BC 04
Appliqué 5: GP 03-C
Appliqué 7: GP 01-P
Block G:
Background: SC 10
Appliqué 1: GP 06-C
Appliqué 3: SC 14
Appliqué 6: GP 09-J
Block H:
Background: SC 09
Appliqué 2: SC 14
Appliqué 4: GP 01-P
Appliqué 5: GP 09-J
Appliqué 7: GP 06-C
Block I:
Background: SC 22
Appliqué 1: GP 09-J

Appliqué 3: GP 03-C
Appliqué 6: BC 04
Block J:
Background: SC 15
Appliqué 2: GP 06-C
Appliqué 4: GP 09-J
Appliqué 5: SC 14
Appliqué 7: GP 03-C
Block K:
Background: SC 13
Appliqué 2: GP 01-P
Appliqué 4: GP 06-C
Appliqué 5: BC 04
Appliqué 7: SC 14
Block L:
Background: SC 21
Appliqué 1: GP 03-C
Appliqué 3: GP 09-J
Appliqué 6: SC 14

Block assembly

blocks A, D, F, H, J, K

a   b

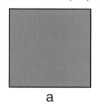 

c   d

e

blocks B, C, E, G, I, L

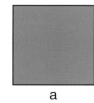

a   b

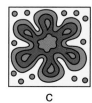

c   d

Wall hanging assembly

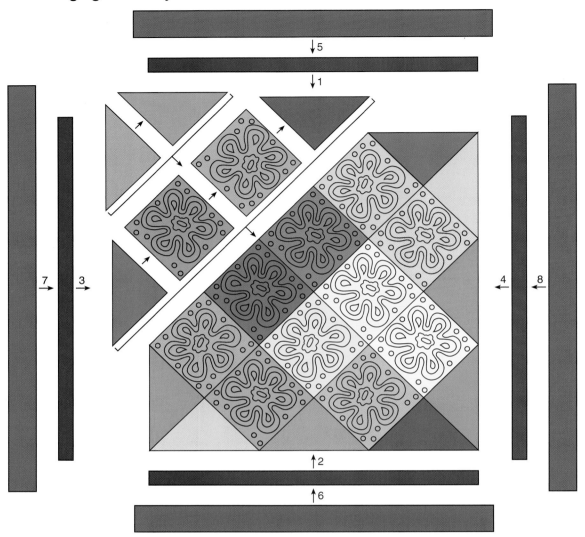

ASSEMBLING THE BLOCKS

Arrange the 12 blocks and 12 triangles into 6 diagonal rows following the wall hanging assembly diagram. Using a ¼in (6mm) seam allowance, join the blocks together into rows, then join the rows together to form the top.

MAKING THE BORDERS

Attach the 2 inner end borders to the edges of the patchwork top and then the side inner borders, using a ¼in (6mm) seam allowance. Repeat the same order with the outer borders.

FINISHING WALL HANGING

Press the assembled patchwork top. Layer the top and backing, and baste together (see page 71). Attach binding to edges (see page 72). Turn to page 73 in the Patchwork Know-how section, for instructions on how to prepare a patchwork for hanging.

Appliqué block key

N.B. See 'Making the Blocks' for details of each block

block A   block B   block C   block D   block E   block F

block G   block H   block I   block J   block K   block L

key

borders and outer triangles

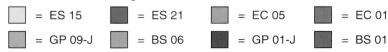

= ES 15   = ES 21   = EC 05   = EC 01

= GP 09-J   = BS 06   = GP 01-J   = BS 01

PATCHWORK KNOW-HOW

These instructions are intended for the novice quilt maker and do not cover all techniques used in making patchwork and patchwork quilts. They provide the basic information needed to make the projects in this book, along with some useful tips. Try not to become overwhelmed by technique, patchwork is a craft which should be enjoyed.

Preparing the fabric

Prewash all new fabrics before you begin, to ensure that there will be no uneven shrinkage and no bleeding of colours when the quilt is laundered. Press the fabric whilst it is still damp to return crispness to the fabric.

Making templates

Templates are best made from transparent template plastic, which is not only durable, but allows you to see the fabric and select certain motifs. You can also make them from thin stiff cardboard if template plastic is not available. If you choose cardboard, paint the edges of the finished template with nail polish to give it longer life.

Templates for machine-piecing

1 Trace off the actual-sized template provided either directly on to template plastic, or tracing paper and then on to thin cardboard. Some of the templates in this book are so large that we have only been able to give you half of them. Before transferring them on to plastic or card, fold a large piece of paper in half. Trace off the half template placing the fold edge up to the fold of the tracing paper, and carefully draw around the shape. Cut out through both thicknesses, and open out for the completed template. Use a ruler to help you trace off the straight cutting line, dotted seam line and grain lines.

2 To cut out the templates use a craft knife, ruler and a self-healing mat.

3 Punch holes in the corners of the template, at each point on the seam line, using a hole punch.

Templates for hand-piecing

• Make a template as shown above, but do not trace off the cutting line. Use the dotted seam line as the outer edge of the template.

• This template allows you to draw the seam lines directly on to the fabric. The seam allowances can then be cut by eye around the patch.

Cutting the fabric

On the individual instructions for each patchwork, you will find a summary of all the patch shapes used.

Always mark and cut out any border and binding strips first, followed by the largest patch shapes and finally the smallest ones, to make the most efficient use of your fabric. The border and binding strips are best cut using a rotary cutter.

Rotary cutting

Rotary cut strips are often cut across the fabric from selvedge to selvedge. With our projects, be certain to cut the strips running in the desired direction.

1 Before beginning to cut, press out any folds or creases in the fabric. If you are cutting a large piece of fabric, you will need to fold it several times to fit the cutting mat. When there is only a single fold, place the fold facing you. If the fabric is too wide to be folded only once, fold it concertina-style until it fits your mat. A small rotary cutter with a sharp blade will cut up to 6 layers of fabric; a large cutter up to 8 layers.

2 To ensure that your cut strips are straight and even, the folds must be placed exactly parallel to the straight edges of the fabric and along a line on the cutting mat.

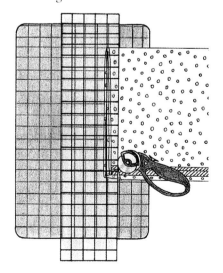

3 Place a plastic ruler over the raw edge of the fabric, overlapping it about ½in (1.25cm). Make sure that the ruler

is at right angles to both the straight edges and the fold to ensure that you cut along the straight grain. Press down on the ruler and wheel the cutter away from yourself along the edge of the ruler.

4 Open out the fabric to check the edge. Don't worry if it's not perfectly straight; a little wiggle will not show when the quilt is stitched together. Re-fold fabric as shown in step 1, then place the ruler over the trimmed edge, aligning edge with the markings on the ruler that match the correct strip width. Cut strip along the edge of the ruler.

Using templates

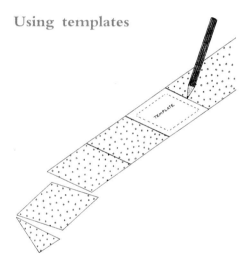

The most efficient way to cut out templates is by first rotary cutting a strip of fabric the width stated for your template and then marking off your templates along the strip, edge to edge at the required angle. This method leaves hardly any waste and gives a random effect to your patches.

A less efficient method is to fussy cut, where the templates are cut individually by placing them on particular motifs or stripes, to create special effects. Although this method is more wasteful it yields very interesting results.

1 Place the template face down on the wrong side of the fabric, with the grain line arrow following the straight grain of the fabric, if indicated. Be careful though - check with your individual instructions, as some instructions may ask you to cut patches on varying grains.

2 Hold the template firmly in place and draw around it with a sharp pencil or crayon, marking in the corner dots or seam lines. To save fabric, position patches close together or even touching. Don't worry if outlines positioned on the straight grain when drawn on striped fabrics do not always match the stripes when cut - this will add a degree of visual excitement to the patchwork!

3 Once you've drawn all the pieces needed, you are ready to cut the fabric, with either a rotary cutter and ruler, or a pair of sharp sewing scissors.

Arranging cut patches

• Quilt instructions always give you a layout for how to arrange the various patch shapes to form the overall geometrical design. It is possible to simply stitch the cut patches together at random, but you will often create a much better effect if you plan the design first.

• Lay the patches out on the floor or stick them to a large flannel or felt covered board, then stand back to study the effect. If you are not happy, swap the patches around until you reach the desired effect.

Basic hand and machine-piecing

Patches can be joined together by hand or machine. Machine stitching is quicker, but hand assembly allows you to carry your patches around with you and work on them in every spare moment. The choice is yours. For techniques that are new to you, practise on scrap pieces of fabric until you feel confident.

Machine-piecing

Follow the quilt instructions for the order in which to piece the individual patchwork blocks and then assemble the blocks together in rows.

1 Seam lines are not marked on the fabric, so stitch $\frac{1}{4}$in (6mm) seams using the machine needle plate and a $\frac{1}{4}$in- (6mm-) wide machine foot, or tape stuck to the machine as a guide. Pin two patches with right sides together,

matching edges. Set your machine at 10-12 stitches per inch (2.5cm) and stitch seams from edge to edge, removing pins as you feed the fabric through the machine.

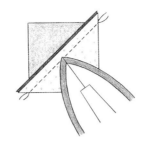

2 Press seams of each patchwork block to one side before joining it to another block.

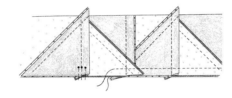

3 When joining rows of blocks, make sure that adjacent seam allowances are pressed in opposite directions to reduce bulk and make matching easier. Pin pieces together directly through the stitch line and to the right and left of the seam. Remove pins as you sew. Continue pressing seams to one side as you work.

Hand-piecing

1 Pin two patches with right sides together, so that the marked seam lines are facing outwards.

2 Using a single strand of strong thread, secure the corner of a seam line with a couple of back stitches.

3 Sew running stitches along the marked line, working 8-10 stitches per inch (2.5cm) and ending at the opposite seam line corner with a few back stitches. When hand piecing never stitch over the seam allowances.

4 Press seams to one side, as shown for machine piecing.

English paper piecing

This is a very easy way to hand assemble a patchwork especially if you are looking for 'travelling' project that you can take with you on vacations or trips.

Cut paper templates from paper of similar weight to the cover of this book. Do not include the seam allowance in these templates. You will need to cut many accurate templates.

Cut the fabric patches roughly $\frac{1}{2}$in (1.25cm) bigger all around than the template. Place the paper templates on to the wrong side of the fabric. Fold the edges of the fabric over the paper, and using large stitches, baste it to the paper. When you have lots of these patches prepared, attach them to each other by holding the pieces right sides together and doing a tiny whipstitch along the edge (see glossary).

Once the patch has been completely attached at all sides you can remove the basting to release the paper. The papers can be reused over and over again until they wrinkle.

Appliqué work

Appliqué is simply a technique of stitching fabric shapes on to a fabric background to create a design. It can be applied by hand, or machine using an invisible blind-hem stitch or decorative embroidery stitches, such as buttonhole or satin stitch.

The method used in this book is machine application. To make the process even easier, the fabric motifs are first fused to the base cloth with an adhesive web, which holds them in place and stops slippage when stitching.

1 Iron paper-backed adhesive web on to the reverse side of your appliqué fabric. If using a template, transfer the appliqué design using dressmakers' carbon paper on to the paper backing, then cut out the design. If using patterns from the fabric print itself, simply cut out the motifs.

2 Peel the paper backing off the motifs, and place them on your fabric in the desired position. Cover with a clean cloth and press motifs in place with a hot iron.

3 Using a contrasting, or complimenting coloured thread, carefully machine-sew small, close zigzag stitches around all edges of the motif, making sure all the raw edges are covered.

Quilting and Finishing

When you have finished piecing your patchwork and have added any borders, press it carefully. It is now ready to be quilted and finished.

Preparing the backing and batting

- Remove the selvedges and piece together the backing fabric to form a backing at least 3in (7.5cm) larger all around than the patchwork top. You won't need to allow quite so much extra fabric around the edges when you are working on a smaller project, such as the baby quilts.

- For quilting choose a fairly thin batting, preferably pure cotton, to give your quilt a flat appearance. If your batting has been rolled up, unroll it and let it rest before cutting it to the same size as the backing.

Basting the layers together

1 On a bare floor or large work surface, lay out the backing with wrong side uppermost. Use weights along the edges keep it taut.

2 Lay the batting on the backing and smooth it out gently. Next lay the patchwork top, right side up, on top of the batting and smooth gently until there are no wrinkles. Pin at the corners and at the mid points of each side, close to the edges.

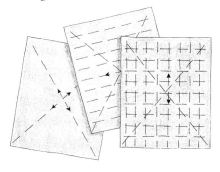

3 Beginning at the centre, baste diagonal lines outwards to the corners, making your stitches about 3in (7.5cm) long. Then, again starting at the centre, baste horizontal and vertical lines out to the edges. Continue basting until you have basted a grid of lines about 4in (10cm) apart over the entire quilt.

4 For speed, when machine quilting, some quilters prefer to baste their quilt sandwich layers together using rust-proof safety pins, spaced at 4in (10cm) intervals over the entire quilt.

Transferring quilting designs and motifs

The tool you use to mark your quilting design on to the fabric must be carefully chosen. Because of the variables of fabric in both colour, texture and fabric surface, no one marker can be recommended. It would be a terrible shame to have made your patchwork quilt up to this stage and then spoil it with bad marking! It is therefore advisable to test out various ways of marking on scrap pieces of fabric, to see how clearly the marks show, and whether any lines that show after stitching can be sponged or washed away. Below is a list of simple but effective ways of tansferring designs.

Chalk-based markers: These include dressmakers' chalk pencils and powered chalk markers. They are available in a variety of colours, and leave a clear line which often disappears during stitching or is easily removed by a brush. Chalk pencils must be kept sharpened to avoid thick lines.

Pencils: Silver and soapstone pencils, available from specialist shops, produce clear lines which are almost invisible after quilting. Coloured pencils can be used on darker fabrics, and water-erasable ones allow the lines to be sponged away after you have completed the stitching.
Pale fabrics present difficulties for marking with pencils. If you choose a lead pencil, make sure it's an 'H' type which will leave only a fine thin line.

Perforating: The design can be transferred from a paper template on to fabric by running a tracing wheel over the lines of the pattern. With many fabrics the indented or perforated line will last long enough for work or a portion of it to be completed.

Dressmakers' carbon paper: The carbon paper is placed working side down, between the paper template and fabric. The design can then be drawn on by tracing around the pattern with a pencil, or running over it with a tracing wheel to produce a dotted line. Dressmakers' carbon is available in a number of colours, for both light and dark fabrics.

Quilters' tape: A narrow re-usable sticky-backed tape, which can be placed onto the fabric surface, to provide a firm guideline for quilting straight-line patterns.

Quilting through paper: Some fabrics are difficult to mark for machine quilting. In these instances the design can be transferred on to tracing paper, which can be pinned to the surface of the quilt. The quilting is then done by stitching through the paper, which is torn away after quilting with the help of a blunt seam ripper.

Templates: Some designs require templates, especially if the pattern is repeated. These can either be used as an aid to help draw patterns directly on to the quilt surface, or when drafting a design full-sized on to paper. With outline templates only the outside of the design can be drawn - any inner details will need to be filled in by hand. Stencil templates can be made at home by transferring the designs on to template plastic, or stiff cardboard. The design is then cut out, to act as guides for both internal and external lines. These templates are a quick method for producing identical repeated designs.

Hand quilting

This is best done with the quilt mounted on a quilting frame or hoop, but as long as you have basted the quilt well a frame is not necessary. With the quilt top facing upwards, begin at the centre of the quilt and make even running stitches following the design. It is more important to make even stitches on both sides of the quilt than to make small ones. Start and finish your stitching with back stitches and bury the ends of your threads in the batting.

Machine quilting

- For a flat looking quilt, always use a walking foot for straight lines, and a darning foot for free-motion quilting.

- It's best to start your quilting at the centre of the quilt and work out towards the borders, doing the straight quilting lines first (stitch-in-the-ditch) followed by the free-motion quilting.

- Make it easier for yourself by handling the quilt properly. Roll up the excess quilt neatly to fit under your sewing machine arm, and use a table or chair to support the weight of the quilt that hangs down the other side.

Preparing to bind the edges

Once you have quilted or tied your quilt sandwich together, remove all the basting stitches. Then, baste around the outer edge of the quilt 1/4in (6mm) from the edge of the top patchwork layer. Trim the back and batting to the edge of the patchwork and straighten the edge of the patchwork if necessary.

Making the binding

1 Cut bias or straight grain strips the width required for your binding, making sure the grainline is running the correct way on your straight grain strips. Cut enough strips until you have the required length to go around the edge of your quilt.

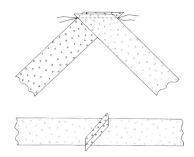

2 To join strips together, the two ends that are to be joined must be cut at a 45 degree angle, as above. Stitch right sides together, trim turnings and press seam open.

Binding the edges

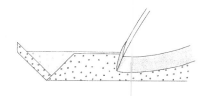

1 Cut the starting end of the binding strip at a 45-degree angle, fold a ¼in (6mm) turning to the wrong side along the cut edge and press in place. With wrong sides together, fold the strip in half lengthways, keeping raw edges level. Press.

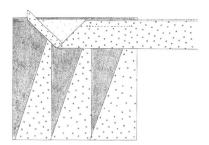

2 Starting at the centre of one of the long edges, place the doubled binding on to the right side of the quilt keeping raw edges level. Stitch the binding in

place starting ¼in (6mm) in from the diagonal folded edge (see below left). Reverse stitch to secure, then work ¼in (6mm) in from the edge of the quilt towards the first corner of the quilt. Stop ¼in (6mm) in from the corner and work a few reverse stitches.

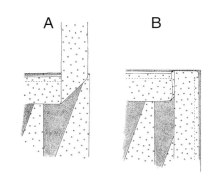

A   B

3 Fold the loose end of the binding up, making a 45-degree angle (see A). Keeping the diagonal fold in place, fold the binding back down, aligning the raw edges with the next side of the quilt. Starting at the point where the last stitch ended, stitch down the next side (see B).

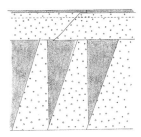

4 Continue to stitch the binding in place around all the quilt edges in this way, tucking the finishing end of the binding inside the diagonal starting section (see above).

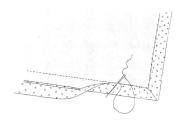

5 Turn the folded edge of the binding on to the back of the quilt. Hand stitch the folded edge in place just covering binding machine stitches, and folding a mitre at each corner.

Completing the Tote bag

Note: Use a ⅜in (1cm) seam allowance throughout and stitch seams with wrong sides together, unless otherwise stated.

1 Stitch the 2 assembled bag sides together down the short side edges. On the plain bag base mark the central point along the 2 short sides with a pin. Matching the side seams on the bag sides to the pins, stitch the sides to the bag base, snipping into the seam turnings on the bag sides at the 4 corners, to help you turn the corner. Repeat with the bag lining sides and base, but leave a large opening in one side seam when stitching the bag lining sides together.

2 With right sides together, place the bag lining inside the bag, matching up the side seams. Stitch together around top edge. Turn bag right sides out, through the opening in the lining side seam. Fold raw edges of opening ⅜in (1cm) to the wrong side and hand slip stitch opening closed. Press seamed top edge flat. Topstitch around top, close to edge keeping seamed edge on the fold.

3 Trim off the selvedges from the 3 strap pieces, and press interfacing to the wrong side of each piece. Stitch the 3 straps together at the short ends to form 1 long strip. Fold strip in half lengthways and stitch long edges together. Turn strap tube through to the right side with the help of a knitting needle or similar pointed object. Press strap flat with seam running centrally along one side.

4 On the base of the bag, start pinning the straps in place following up one vertical patchwork seam on the bag side, keeping the strap seam hidden below. Measure off approximately 29in (74cm) of strap above top of bag for the loose strap, and then on the same bag side, continue pinning down the second patchwork seam to the base. Pin strap across base and onto second bag side in the same manner, finishing off at the starting point. Trim off any excess strap and tuck in raw ends. Stitch in place down both side edges of straps and across straps at top edge of bag.

5 Totally cover the cardboard base stiffener with fabric, then glue or stitch in place. Place stiffener inside base of bag with seams to the underside.

Completing
the Pillowcase

Note: Use a ³/₈in (1cm) seam allowance throughout and stitch seams with wrong sides together, unless otherwise stated.

1 Neaten one long edge of the facing, then with raw edges level stitch the facing to one bordered edge of the front pillowcase, with a ¼in (6mm) seam allowance. Press facing on to wrong side of front pillowcase and topstitch in place by working a row of stitching following the border seamline.

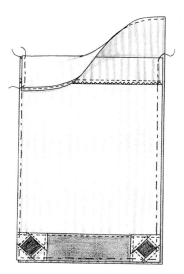

2 Neaten one short edge of the back pillowcase by pressing a double turned ¼in (6mm) hem to the wrong side. Stitch in place. Place front and back pillowcases together, keeping raw edges level and letting the hemmed edge of the back extend out above the faced end of the front pillowcase. Baste raw edges together, then fold the back hemmed section over on to the front pillowcase to cover the faced section. Baste in place at the sides. Machine stitch together around the tacked sides. Neaten edges, and turn cover through to right side. Press seamed edges flat.

Completing
the Duvet

Note: Use a ³/₈in (1cm) seam allowance throughout and stitch seams with wrong sides together, unless otherwise stated.

1 Stitch the 2 backing pieces together to form 1 piece measuring 74½in x 54½in (189cm x 138cm) for a single bed, and 74½in x 84½in (189cm x 215cm) for a double.

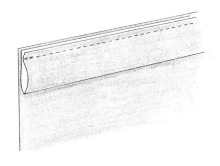

2 Fold the wider facing in half along its length to form a strip 2½in- (6.5cm-) wide. Baste facing raw edges together, then baste the facing to the right side of the duvet backing along one edge, keeping raw edges level. Stitch in place, then press facing over onto wrong side of backing.

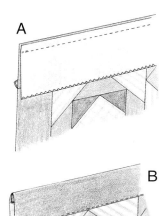

3 Neaten one long edge of the narrow facing, then with raw edges level stitch the facing to one edge of the patchwork top with a ¼in (6mm) seam allowance (see A). Press facing on to wrong side of patchwork top and topstitch in place by working a row of stitching following the border seamline (see B). For a single bed work 4 equally spaced buttonholes along the faced border edge of the patchwork top and for a double work 6 buttonholes.

4 Open out the facing on the duvet backing and place the patchwork front onto the backing, with the faced and buttonholed edge up to the facing seamline on the backing.

In the same way as the pillowcase baste the 3 raw edges together, and then fold the backing facing over on to the patchwork front to cover the buttonhole facing. Baste in place at the sides.

Machine stitch together around the tacked sides. Neaten edges, and turn cover through to right side.

Press seamed edges flat and stitch buttons to back facing to correspond with the buttonholes.

Completing
the Cushion covers

Note: Use a ³/₈in (1cm) seam allowance throughout and stitch seams with wrong sides together, unless otherwise stated.

1 Bind one long edge of the 2 cushion backs (see page 72). Lay the cushion top face up on a flat surface and place one back face down on top, with raw edges level and bound edge towards the centre. Place the second back face down on top of the uncovered side of the cushion top, keeping raw edges level and overlapping the bound edges at the centre.

2 Baste the cushion cover pieces together around all sides and machine stitch together. Turn cover through to right side and insert cushion pad through centre back opening.

How to prepare
a Patchwork or
Quilt for hanging

To keep your patchwork flat when hanging on a wall, it's best to inset wooden dowels through channels at the top and base of the hanging. To do this cut 2 strips of any fabric (although fabric that matches the backing will look best) 1³/₄in- (4.5cm-) x width of hanging.

Press all raw edges of each strip ³/₈in (1cm) to the wrong side, and then slipstitch the strips to the wrong side of the hanging at the top and base, along the long pressed edges.

Insert long wooden dowels 1¼in (3cm) shorter than width of hanging and slipstitch ends of channels closed.

To hang the wall hanging stitch a brass ring to each end of top channel and use to hook them over picture hooks, or nails.

THE KAFFE FASSETT FABRIC COLLECTION

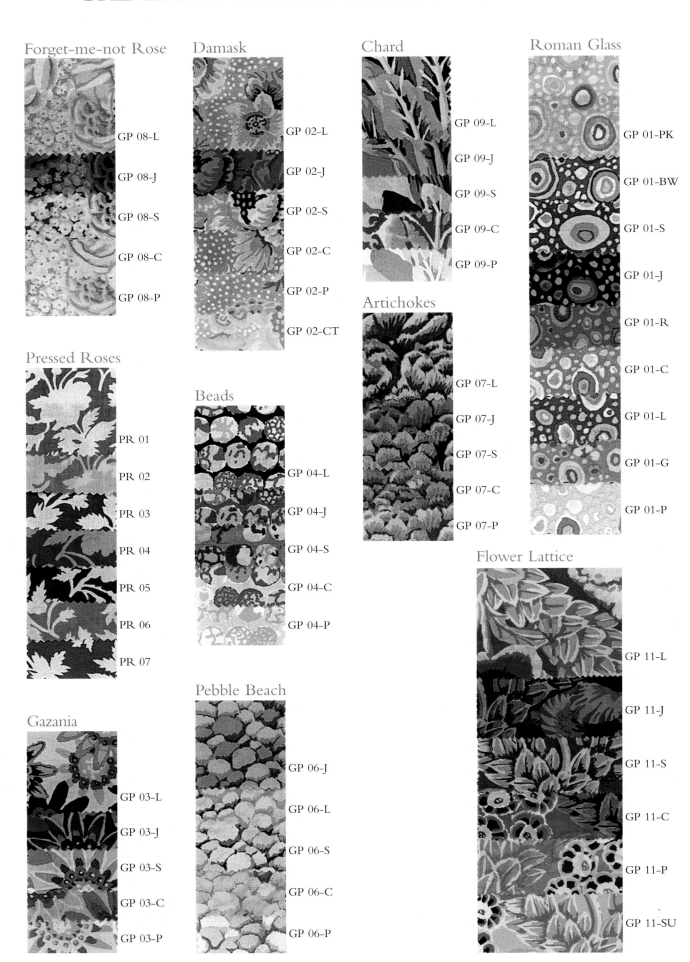

Forget-me-not Rose

GP 08-L
GP 08-J
GP 08-S
GP 08-C
GP 08-P

Damask

GP 02-L
GP 02-J
GP 02-S
GP 02-C
GP 02-P
GP 02-CT

Chard

GP 09-L
GP 09-J
GP 09-S
GP 09-C
GP 09-P

Roman Glass

GP 01-PK
GP 01-BW
GP 01-S
GP 01-J
GP 01-R
GP 01-C
GP 01-L
GP 01-G
GP 01-P

Pressed Roses

PR 01
PR 02
PR 03
PR 04
PR 05
PR 06
PR 07

Beads

GP 04-L
GP 04-J
GP 04-S
GP 04-C
GP 04-P

Artichokes

GP 07-L
GP 07-J
GP 07-S
GP 07-C
GP 07-P

Flower Lattice

GP 11-L
GP 11-J
GP 11-S
GP 11-C
GP 11-P
GP 11-SU

Gazania

GP 03-L
GP 03-J
GP 03-S
GP 03-C
GP 03-P

Pebble Beach

GP 06-J
GP 06-L
GP 06-S
GP 06-C
GP 06-P

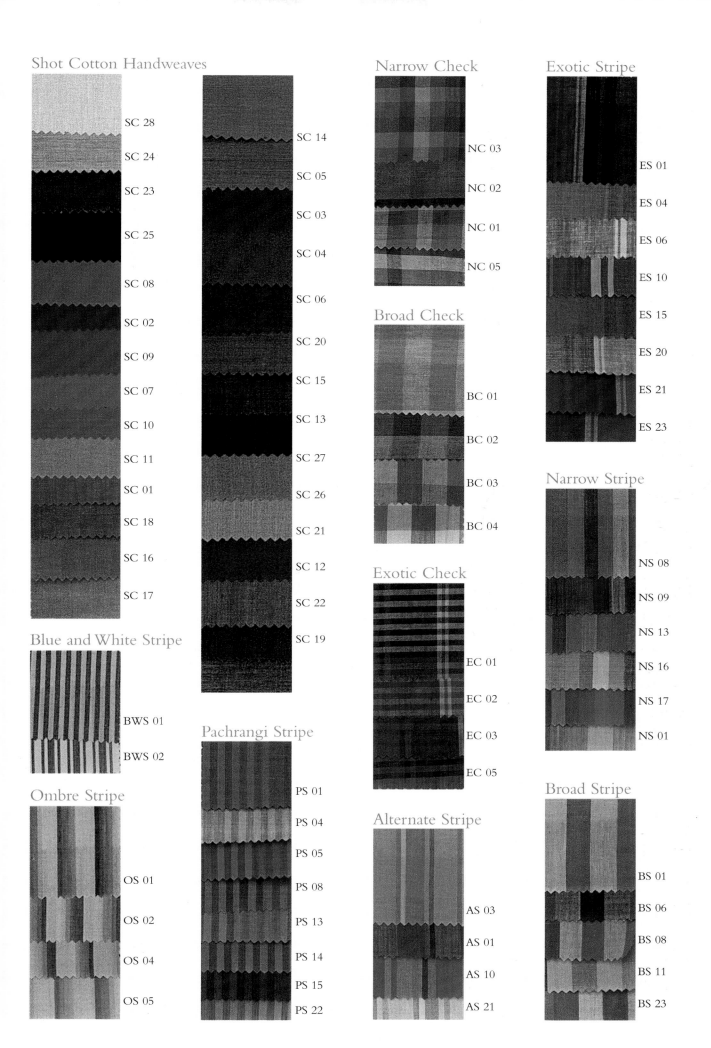

Shot Cotton Handweaves

SC 28
SC 24
SC 23
SC 25
SC 08
SC 02
SC 09
SC 07
SC 10
SC 11
SC 01
SC 18
SC 16
SC 17

SC 14
SC 05
SC 03
SC 04
SC 06
SC 20
SC 15
SC 13
SC 27
SC 26
SC 21
SC 12
SC 22
SC 19

Blue and White Stripe

BWS 01
BWS 02

Ombre Stripe

OS 01
OS 02
OS 04
OS 05

Pachrangi Stripe

PS 01
PS 04
PS 05
PS 08
PS 13
PS 14
PS 15
PS 22

Narrow Check

NC 03
NC 02
NC 01
NC 05

Broad Check

BC 01
BC 02
BC 03
BC 04

Exotic Check

EC 01
EC 02
EC 03
EC 05

Alternate Stripe

AS 03
AS 01
AS 10
AS 21

Exotic Stripe

ES 01
ES 04
ES 06
ES 10
ES 15
ES 20
ES 21
ES 23

Narrow Stripe

NS 08
NS 09
NS 13
NS 16
NS 17
NS 01

Broad Stripe

BS 01
BS 06
BS 08
BS 11
BS 23

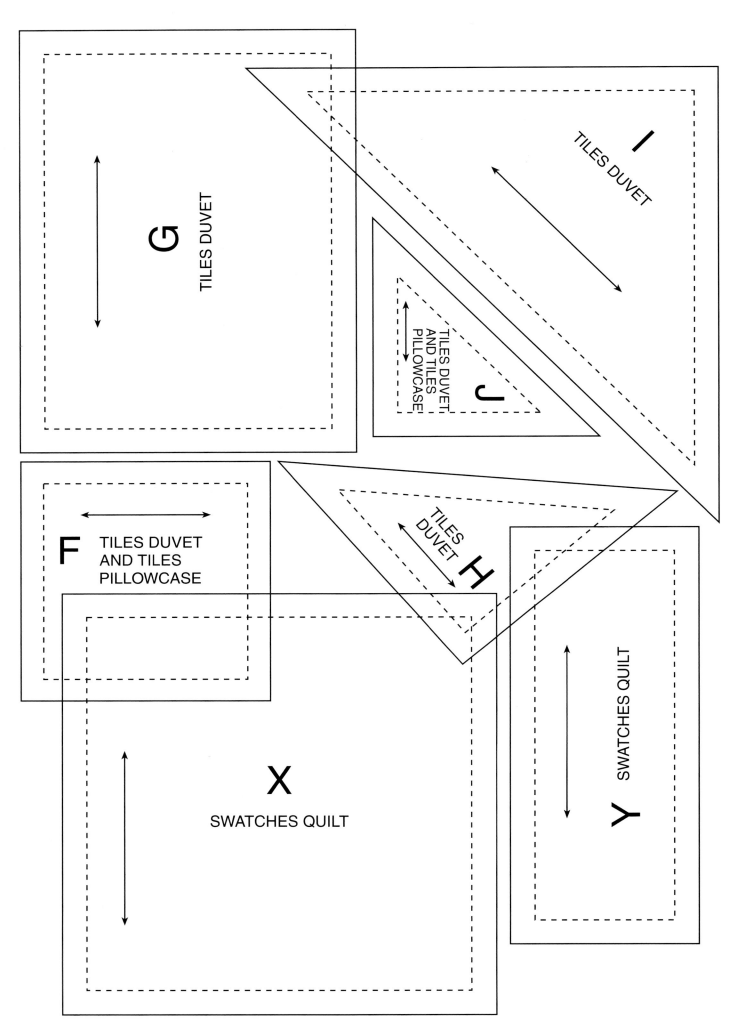

G
TILES DUVET

I
TILES DUVET

J
TILES DUVET
AND TILES
PILLOWCASE

F
TILES DUVET
AND TILES
PILLOWCASE

H
TILES
DUVET

X
SWATCHES QUILT

Y
SWATCHES QUILT

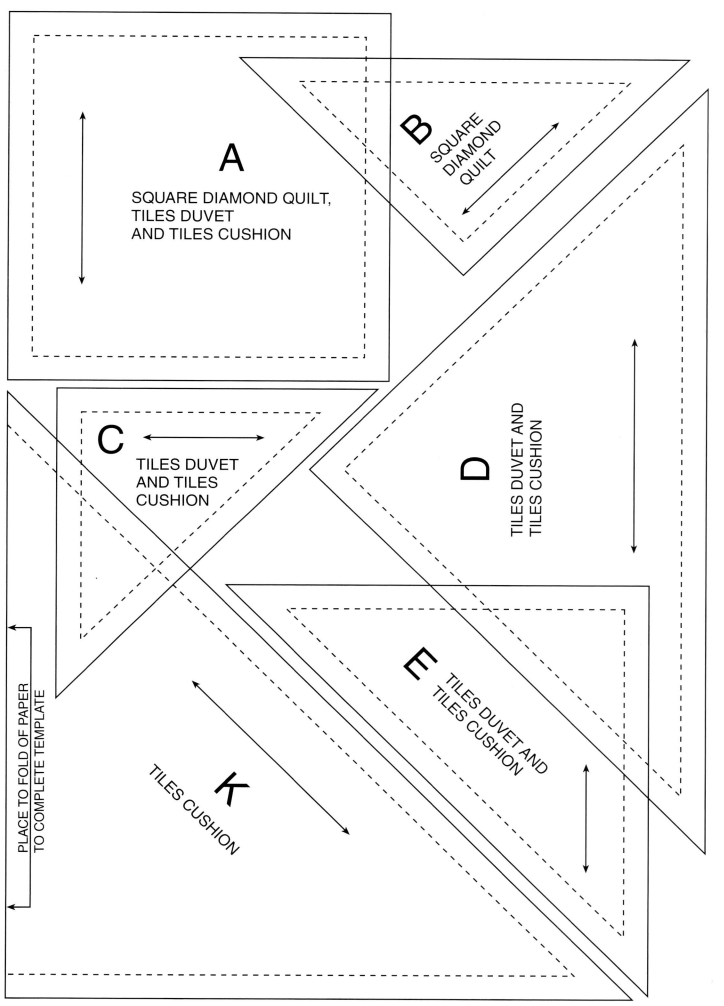

A

SQUARE DIAMOND QUILT,
TILES DUVET
AND TILES CUSHION

B SQUARE DIAMOND QUILT

C

TILES DUVET
AND TILES
CUSHION

D

TILES DUVET AND
TILES CUSHION

E TILES DUVET AND
TILES CUSHION

K

TILES CUSHION

PLACE TO FOLD OF PAPER
TO COMPLETE TEMPLATE

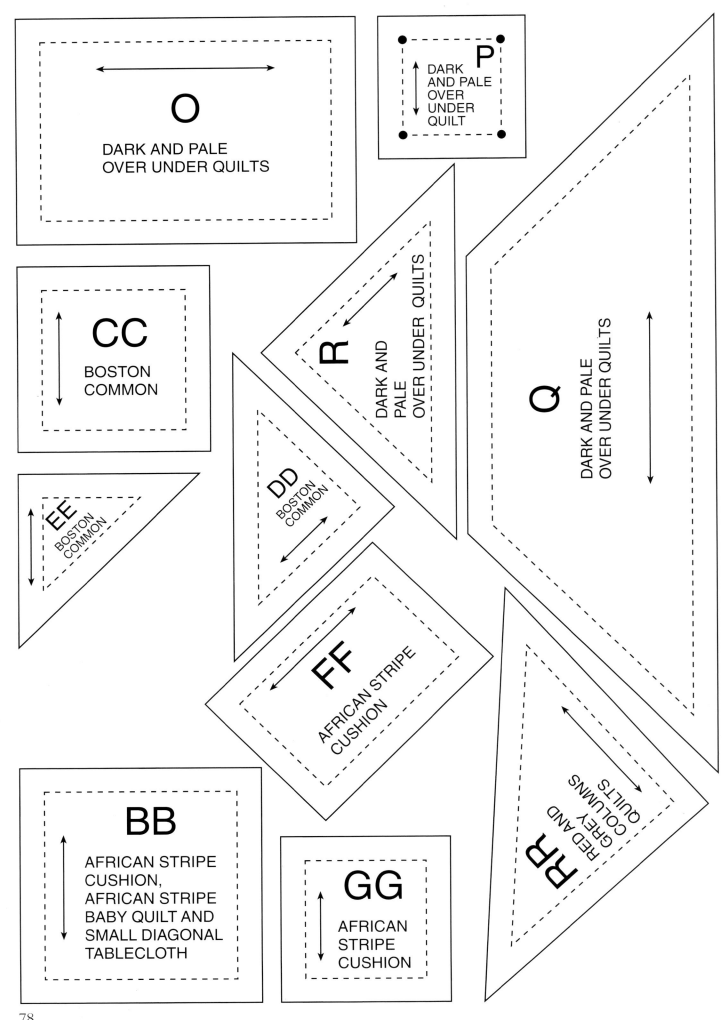

O
DARK AND PALE
OVER UNDER QUILTS

P
DARK
AND PALE
OVER
UNDER
QUILT

CC
BOSTON
COMMON

R
DARK
AND PALE
OVER UNDER QUILTS

Q
DARK AND PALE
OVER UNDER QUILTS

EE
BOSTON
COMMON

DD
BOSTON
COMMON

FF
AFRICAN STRIPE
CUSHION

BB
AFRICAN STRIPE
CUSHION,
AFRICAN STRIPE
BABY QUILT AND
SMALL DIAGONAL
TABLECLOTH

GG
AFRICAN
STRIPE
CUSHION

RR
RED AND
GREY
COLUMNS
QUILTS

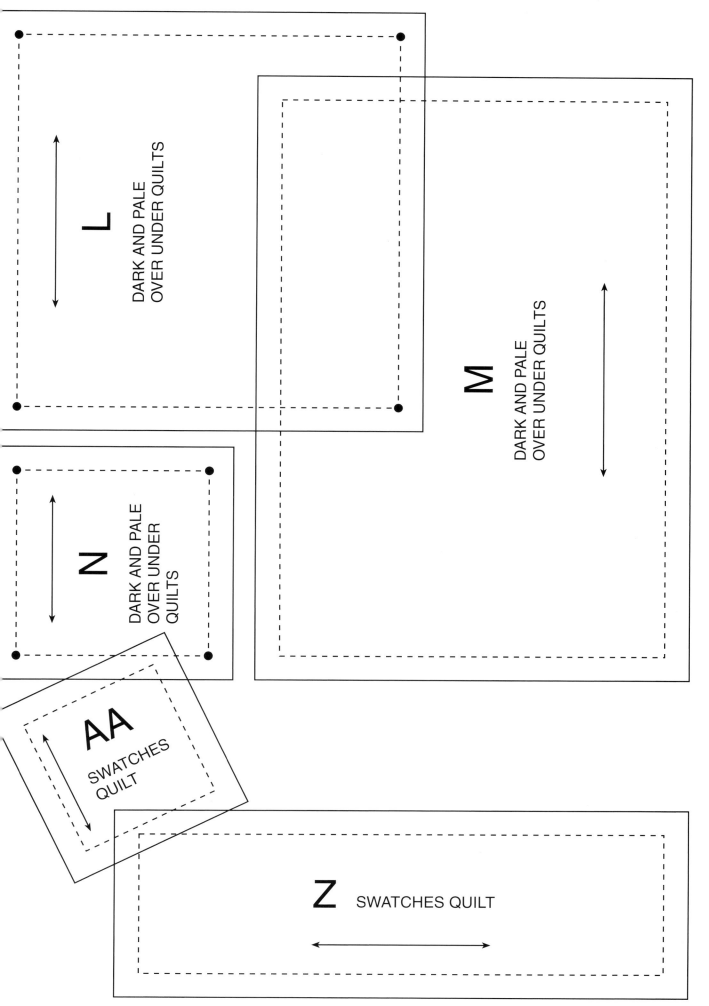

L

DARK AND PALE
OVER UNDER QUILTS

M

DARK AND PALE
OVER UNDER QUILTS

N

DARK AND PALE
OVER UNDER
QUILTS

AA

SWATCHES
QUILT

Z SWATCHES QUILT

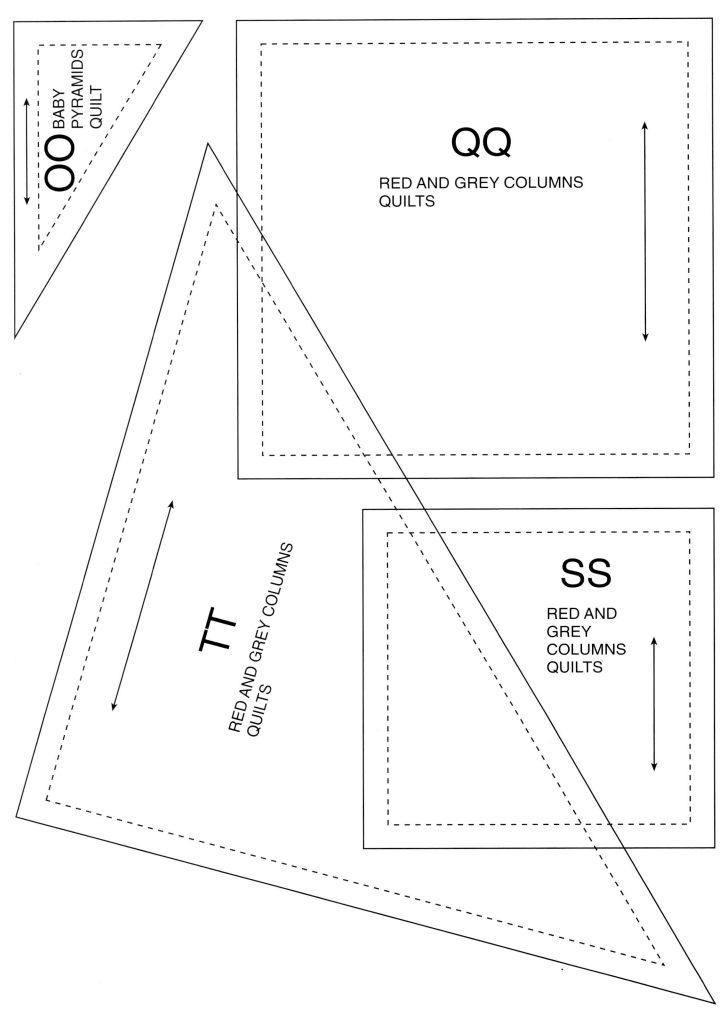

OO BABY PYRAMIDS QUILT

QQ
RED AND GREY COLUMNS QUILTS

TT
RED AND GREY COLUMNS QUILTS

SS
RED AND GREY COLUMNS QUILTS

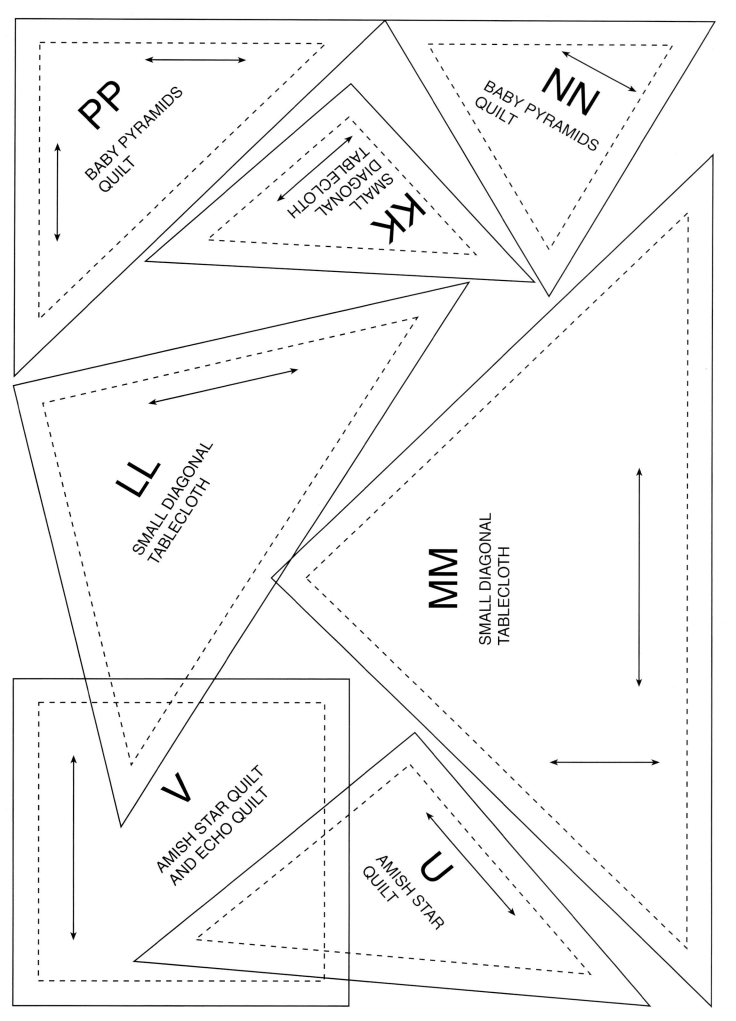

PP
BABY PYRAMIDS
QUILT

NN
BABY PYRAMIDS
QUILT

KK
SMALL
DIAGONAL
TABLECLOTH

LL
SMALL DIAGONAL
TABLECLOTH

MM
SMALL DIAGONAL
TABLECLOTH

V
AMISH STAR QUILT
AND ECHO QUILT

U
AMISH STAR
QUILT

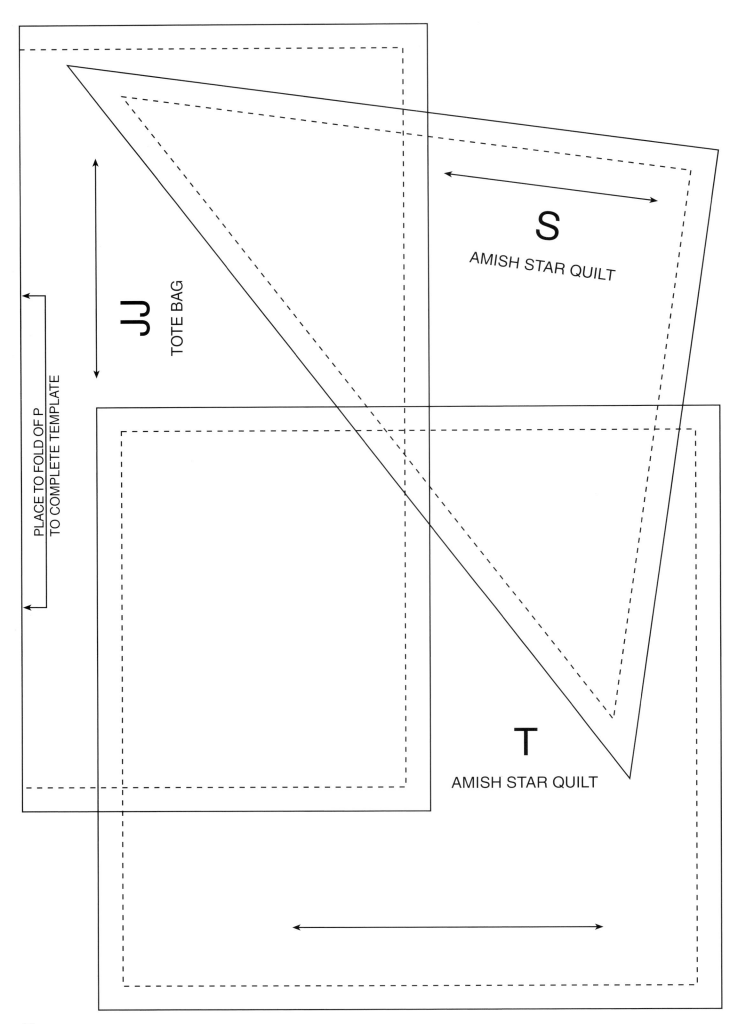

S

AMISH STAR QUILT

JJ

TOTE BAG

PLACE TO FOLD OF P
TO COMPLETE TEMPLATE

T

AMISH STAR QUILT

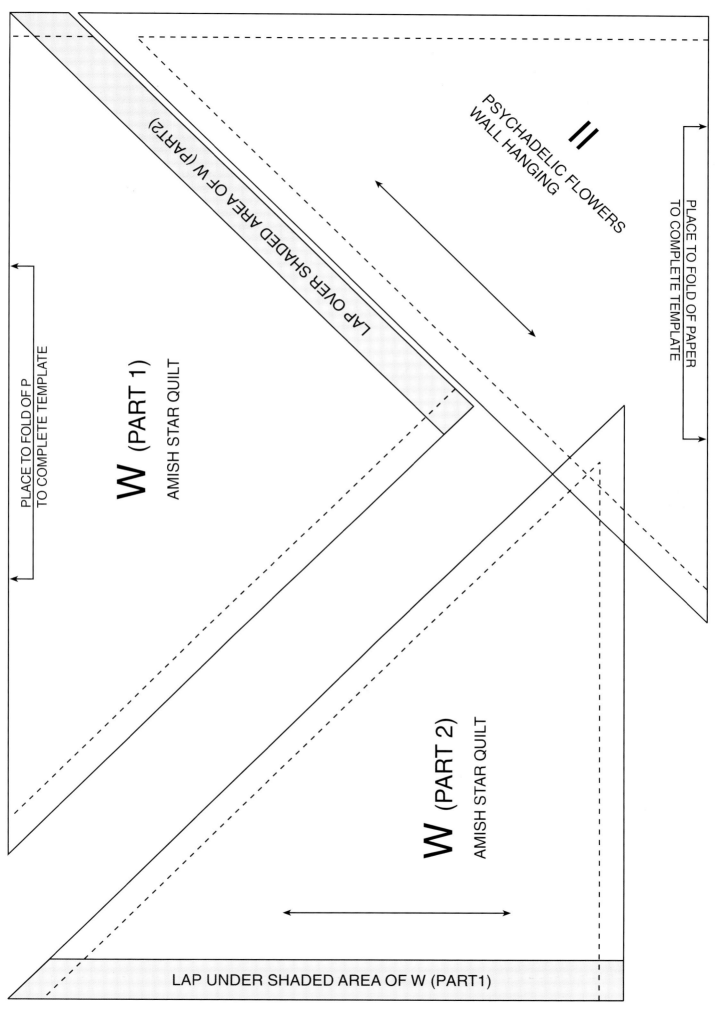

PSYCHADELIC FLOWERS
WALL HANGING

W (PART 1)
AMISH STAR QUILT

W (PART 2)
AMISH STAR QUILT

LAP OVER SHADED AREA OF W (PART2)

LAP UNDER SHADED AREA OF W (PART1)

PLACE TO FOLD OF P
TO COMPLETE TEMPLATE

PLACE TO FOLD OF PAPER
TO COMPLETE TEMPLATE

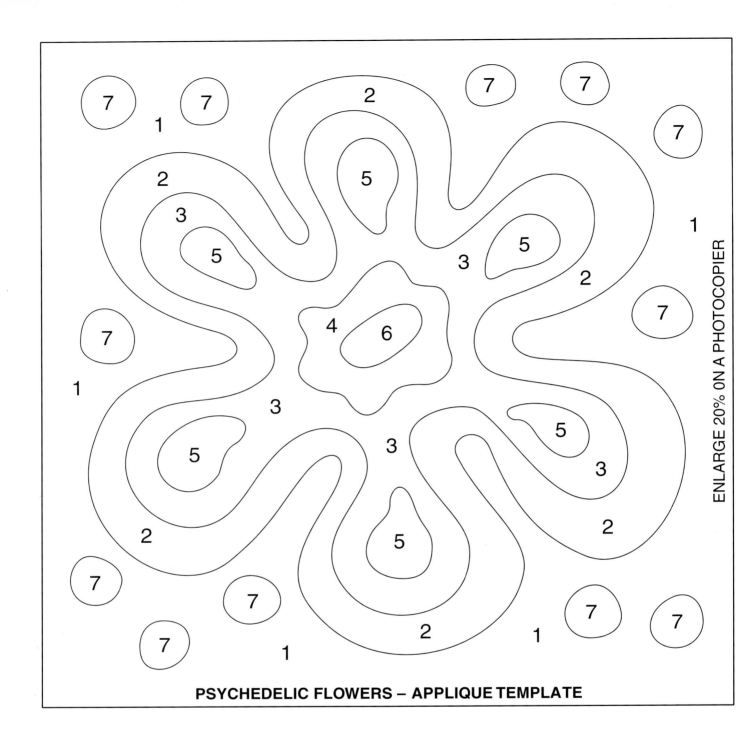

PSYCHEDELIC FLOWERS – APPLIQUE TEMPLATE

ENLARGE 20% ON A PHOTOCOPIER

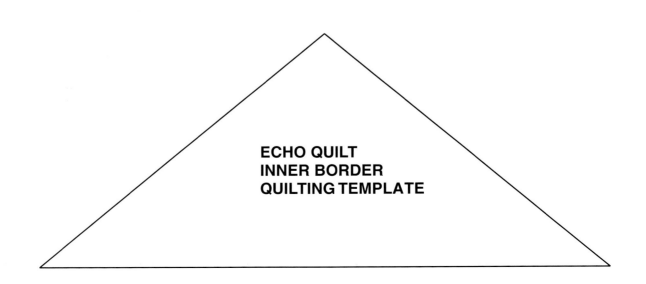

**ECHO QUILT
INNER BORDER
QUILTING TEMPLATE**

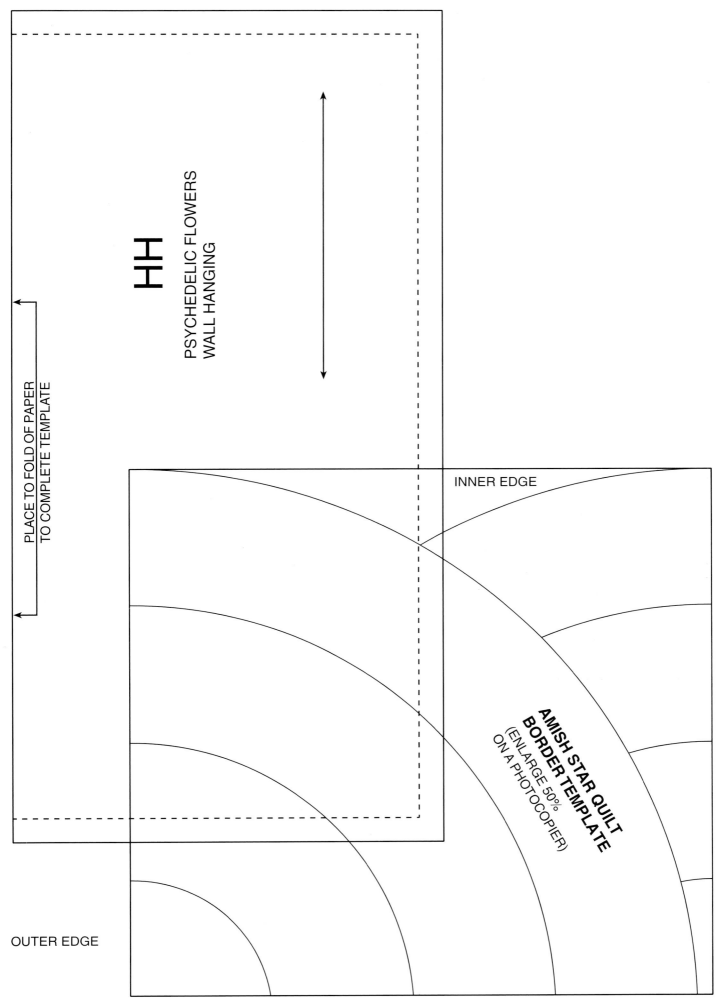

HH

PSYCHEDELIC FLOWERS
WALL HANGING

PLACE TO FOLD OF PAPER
TO COMPLETE TEMPLATE

INNER EDGE

AMISH STAR QUILT
BORDER TEMPLATE
(ENLARGE 50%
ON A PHOTOCOPIER)

OUTER EDGE

RED COLUMNS QUILT – TRIANGULAR TEMPLATE

GREY COLUMNS QUILT – INNER BORDER LEAF TEMPLATE

**RED COLUMNS QUILT
DAISY MOTIF**

GLOSSARY OF TERMS

Appliqué The technique of stitching fabric shapes on to a background to create a design. It can be applied either by hand or machine with a decorative embroidery stitch, such as buttonhole, or satin stitch.

Backing The bottom layer of a *quilt sandwich*. It is made of fabric pieced to the size of the quilt top with the addition of about 3in (7.5cm) all around to allow for quilting take-up.

Basting Also known as tacking in Britain. This is a means of holding two fabric layers or the layers of a *quilt sandwich* together temporarily with large hand stitches, or pins.

Batting Also known as wadding in Britain, batting or *padding* is the middle layer of a quilt sandwich. It can be made of cotton, wool, silk or synthetic fibres and can be bought in sheets or as a loose stuffing.

Bias The diagonal *grain* of a fabric. This is the direction which has the most give or stretch, making it ideal for bindings, especially on curved edges.

Binding A narrow strip of fabric used to finish off the edges of quilts or projects; it can be cut on the straight *grain* of a fabric or on the *bias*.

Block A single design unit that when stitched together with other blocks creates the quilt top. It is most often a square, hexagon, or rectangle, but it can be any shape. It can be pieced or plain.

Border A frame of fabric stitched to the outer edges of the quilt top. Borders can be narrow or wide, pieced or plain. As well as making the quilt larger, they unify the overall design and draw attention to the central area.

Butted corner A corner finished by stitching *border* strips together at right angles to each other.

Chalk pencils Are available in various colours, they are used for marking lines or spots on fabric. Some pencils have a brush attached to one end, although marks are easily removed.

Cutting mat Designed for use with a *rotary cutter*, it is made from a special 'self-healing' material that keeps your cutting blade sharp. Cutting mats come in various sizes and are usually marked with a grid to help you line up the edges of fabric and cut out larger pieces.

Darning foot A specialist sewing machine foot that is used in *free-motion* quilting – the *feed dogs* are disengaged so that stitches can be worked in varying lengths and directions.

Ditch quilting Also known as *quilting-in-the-ditch* or *stitch-in-the-ditch*. The quilting stitches are worked along the actual seam lines which hold the patches together, to give a *pieced quilt* texture. This is a particularly good technique for beginners as the stitches cannot be seen – only their effect.

Dressmakers' carbon paper Sometimes sold as tracing paper. Available in a number of colours, for light or dark fabric. It can be used with pencils or a tracing wheel to transfer a quilting or appliqué design on to fabric.

English paper piecing An easy hand method of piecing a patchwork together. With this method you baste each patch to an individual paper template, folding the seam allowances onto the wrong side. The patches, still mounted on the paper, are then stitched together before the paper is removed.

Feed dogs The part of a sewing machine located within the *needle plate* which rhythmically moves up and down to help move the fabric along while sewing.

Free-motion quilting Curved wavy quilting lines stitched in a random manner. Stitching diagrams are often given as a very loose guide.

Fussy cutting This is when a template is placed on a particular motif, or stripe, to obtain interesting effects. This method is not as efficient as strip cutting, but can yield striking results.

Grain The direction in which the threads run in a woven fabric. In a vertical direction it is called the lengthwise grain, and has very little stretch. The horizontal direction, or crosswise grain is slightly stretchy, but diagonally the fabric has a lot of stretch. This diagonal grain is called the *bias*. Wherever possible the grain of a fabric should run in the same direction on a quilt *block* and *borders*.

Iron-on interfacing eg. Vilene/Pellon. A non-woven supporting material with adhesive that melts when ironed, making the interfacing adhere to the fabric.

Mitred corner A corner finished by folding and stitching the binding strip neatly at a 45-degree angle.

Needle plate The metal plate on a sewing machine, through which the needle passes via a hole to the lower part of the machine. They are often marked with lines at $1/4$in (5mm) intervals, to use as stitching guides.

Padding Also known as *batting* in the United states and *wadding* in Britain, this is the middle layer of a *quilt sandwich*. Padding can be made of cotton, wool, silk or synthetic fibres and can be bought in sheets or as a loose stuffing.

Paper-backed adhesive web eg. Bondaweb/Wonder-Under. It is cut to shape, pressed to the wrong side of a fabric shape using a hot iron, and the paper backing is peeled off. The fabric shape can then be placed on top of another piece of fabric, adhesive side down, and pressed into place.

Patch A small shaped piece of fabric used in the making of a *patchwork* pattern.

Patchwork The technique of stitching small pieces of fabric (*patches*) together to create a larger piece of fabric, usually forming a design.

Pieced quilt A quilt composed of *patches*.

Pins Use good quality pins. Do not use thick, burred or rusted pins which will leave holes or marks. Long pins with glass or plastic heads are easier to use when pinning through thick fabrics. Safety pins (size 2) can be used to 'pin-baste' the quilt layers together.

Quilters' tape A narrow removable masking tape. If placed lightly on fabric, it provides a firm guideline for straight-line patterns.

Quilting Traditionally done by hand with running stitches, but for speed modern quilts are often stitched by machine. The stitches are sewn through the top, *padding* and *backing*, to hold the three layers together. Quilting stitches are usually worked in some form of design, but they can be random.

Quilting foot See *walking foot*.

Quilting frame A free-standing wooden frame in which the quilt layers are fixed for the entire quilting process. Provides the most even surface for quilting.

Quilting hoop Consists of two wooden circular or oval rings with a screw adjuster on the outer ring. It stabilises the quilt layers, helping to create an even tension.

Quilt sandwich Comprised of three layers of fabric: a decorative top, a middle lining or *padding* and a *backing*. Collectively these are known as the 'quilt sandwich'. They are held together with the quilting stitches or individual ties.

Rotary cutter A sharp circular blade attached to a handle for quick, accurate cutting. It is a device that can be used to cut up to six layers of fabric at one time. It needs to be used in conjunction with a 'self-healing' *cutting mat* and a thick plastic *rotary ruler*.

Rotary ruler A thick, clear plastic ruler printed with lines that are exactly 1/4in (6mm) apart. Sometimes they also have diagonal lines printed on, indicating 45 and 60-degree angles. A rotary ruler is used as a guide when cutting out fabric pieces using a *rotary cutter*.

Selvedges Also known as *selvages*, these are the firmly woven edges down each side of a fabric length. Selvedges should be trimmed off before cutting out your fabric, as they are more liable to shrink when the fabric is washed. They are also difficult to quilt due to the firm nature of the weave.

Stitch-in-the-ditch See *ditch quilting*.

Template A pattern piece used as a guide for marking and cutting out fabric *patches*, or marking a *quilting*, or *appliqué* design. Usually made from plastic or strong card that can be reused many times.

Threads 100 percent cotton or cotton-covered polyester is best for hand and machine piecing. Choose a colour that matches your fabric. When sewing different colours and patterns together, choose a medium to light neutral colour, such as gray or ecru. For both hand and machine *quilting* it helps to use coated or pre-waxed quilting thread, which allows the thread to glide through the quilt layers. Hand quilting can be worked in special threads, such as pearl or crochet cotton.

Tracing wheel A tool consisting of a spiked wheel attached to a handle. It can be used to transfer a quilting design from paper on to fabric, by running the wheel over the design lines.

Wadding The British term for *batting*, or *padding*.

Walking foot Also known as a *quilting foot*, this is a sewing machine foot with dual feed control. It is very helpful when quilting, as the fabric layers are fed evenly from the top and below, reducing the risk of slippage and puckering.

Whipstitch Small, even hand stitches used to join two finished edges as, for example, when attaching patches together in *English paper piecing*. The patches are placed right sides facing, with neatened edges level. Working along the top edges, insert a needle close to the edge from the back through to the front, picking up just a few threads. Draw sewing thread through. Continue in this manner, keeping stitches uniform in size and spacing until edges are joined.

INDEX

KAFFE FASSETT FABRICS

Alternate stripe
  AS 01: 42, 44
  AS 03: 56
  AS 10: 40, 42, 56
  AS 21: 40, 46, 52, 56
Artichokes
  GP 07-P: 50,54
  GP 07-S: 50, 54
  GP 07-L: 50
  GP 07-C: 54
  GP 07-J:56
Beads
  GP 04-J: 50
  GP 04-S: 50
Blue and white stripe
  BWS 01: 48, 50, 52
  BWS 02: 34, 38, 39, 48, 50, 52
Broad check
  BC 01: 40, 52, 63
  BC 02: 32, 42
  BC 04: 40, 41, 66, 67
Broad stripe
  BS 01: 40, 41, 42, 44, 46, 56, 57, 67
  BS06: 42, 44, 61, 66
  BS 08: 44
  BS 11: 40, 41, 46
  BS 23: 42
Chard
  GP 09-S: 54
  GP 09-J: 66
Damask
  GP 02-P: 50, 54
  GP 02-S: 50, 54
  GP 02-C: 50, 54
  GP 02-J: 56
Exotic check
  EC 01: 42, 54, 66
  EC 03: 32
  EC 05: 66
Exotic stripe
  ES 04: 54
  ES 10: 42
  ES 15: 42, 54, 56, 66

ES 20: 46
ES 21: 42, 66
ES 23: 32
Flower lattice
  GP 11-S: 54
  GP 11-C: 56
Forget Me Not Rose
  GP 08-J: 56
Gazania
  GP 03-S: 50, 54
  GP 03-J: 61
  GP 03-C: 66
Narrow check
  NC 01: 36, 54
  NC 02: 34, 39
  NC 03: 56
  NC 05: 32
Narrow stripe
  NS 01: 37, 42, 44, 46, 61
  NS 08: 32, 42, 44
  NS 09: 42, 44
  NS 13: 42, 44, 46
  NS 16: 46, 52, 57
  NS 17: 42, 44, 56
Ombre stripe
  OS 01: 36, 46, 48, 52
  OS 02: 46, 48, 52, 54
  OS 04: 46, 48
  OS 05: 36, 37,46, 48, 50, 52, 54
Pachrangi stripe
  PS 01: 42, 44
  PS 04: 36, 40, 42, 46, 52
  PS 08: 44, 58
  PS 13: 40, 42, 44, 56
  PS 14: 40
  PS 15: 42, 44
  PS 22: 40, 41, 42, 44, 46
Pebble beach
  GP 06-J: 36, 50
  GP 06-S: 50
  GP 06-C: 66
Pressed Roses
  PR 01: 36, 54

PR 02: 36
PR 03: 36
PR 04: 36, 56
PR 05: 36
PR 06: 36, 56
PR 07: 36, 37, 54
Roman glass
  GP 01-G: 36, 46, 50, 56
  GP 01-BW: 36, 54
  GP 01-PK: 36
  GP 01-S: 36, 50, 54
  GP 01-R: 56
  GP 01-L: 61
  GP 01-P: 66
  GP 01-J: 67
Shot cotton
  SC 01: 44
  SC 02: 40, 64, 66
  SC 03: 58, 66
  SC 05: 34, 38, 48, 58
  SC 06: 34, 39
  SC 07: 44, 66
  SC 08: 34, 38, 39, 44
  SC 09: 44, 56, 66
  SC 10: 58, 66
  SC 11: 44, 48, 58
  SC 12: 44, 58
  SC 13: 66
  SC 14: 37, 44, 48, 54, 58, 61, 63, 66
  SC 15: 32, 34, 38, 66
  SC 16: 44, 61
  SC 17: 48, 61
  SC 18: 32, 40, 58
  SC 19: 32, 61
  SC 20: 32, 34, 39, 44, 61
  SC 21: 44, 61, 66
  SC 22: 42, 61, 66
  SC 23: 63, 64
  SC 24: 52, 62, 64
  SC 25: 64
  SC 26: 44, 48
  SC 27: 52, 54
  SC 28: 62

All fabrics are listed on page 31, 74, 75